THE COUNSELOR
AS CONSULTANT AND
SUPERVISOR

THE COUNSELOR AS CONSULTANT AND SUPERVISOR

By

VICTOR J. DRAPELA, Ph.D.

Professor and Chairman
Counselor Education Department
University of South Florida
Tampa, Florida

WITH A FOREWORD BY

Garry R. Walz, Ph.D.

Professor of Counselor Education
Director of ERIC/CAPS Clearinghouse
School of Education
The University of Michigan
Ann Arbor, Michigan

CHARLES C THOMAS • PUBLISHER

Springfield • Illinois • U.S.A.

Published and Distributed Throughout the World by

CHARLES C THOMAS • PUBLISHER
2600 South First Street
Springfield, Illinois, 62717, U.S.A.

© *1983 by* CHARLES C THOMAS • PUBLISHER

ISBN 0-398-04789-8

Library of Congress Catalog Card Number: 82-19315

Printed in the United States of America

I-R-1

Library of Congress Cataloging in Publication Data

Drapela, Victor J.
    The counselor as consultant and supervisor.

    Bibliography: p.
    Includes index.
    1. Counseling. 2. Psychological consultation. 3. Coun-
selors--Supervision of. I. Title.
BF637.C6D658   1983   158'.3   82-19315
ISBN 0-398-04789-8

This book is dedicated to the many graduate students in counselor education who have enriched my life and, in particular, to one who has later become my wife and best friend,

GWEN BLAVAT DRAPELA

FOREWORD

THE early years of counseling were years of exploration and experimentation with the dynamic power of the counseling relationship. Initially, we thought that the counselors' major contribution to their clients was acting as expert diagnosticians, individuals who, like their clinical counterparts in medicine, provided skillful diagnosis through the use of tests. With time, the realization of the power and potential of the counseling relationship expanded our boundaries. The recognition that the counseling relationship provided the climate in which clients, with the unconditional positive regard of their counselors, could confront their problems, thus directly opening their lives to alternative responses and behaviors, established the individual counseling model. The admitted success of this individual counseling model and its widespread proponents subtly shaped and influenced our thinking and behavior. In writings and actions, counselors collectively defined the counselor's role as that of counseling. In effect, the more time counselors were able to spend working with individual clients, the more they were fulfilling the role of counselor and the more they were lauded for their efforts.

The acceptance of the individual model clearly marked the breakdown of existing resistances to individual counseling. It also provided a protection of sorts against the performance of relatively unimportant quasi-administrative and management functions that take up so much precious time. Unfortunately, it also had the negative effect of binding counselors to a single intervention, counseling, and limiting their growth and involvement in broader areas of helping interventions. They failed to move into the environment in which clients lived and behaved.

In this volume, Dr. Drapela has taken a major step toward helping counselors reconceptualize their roles and define them more broadly. A variety of intervention strategies and methods are used to illustrate these roles. His perspective is a very welcomed one as we try to redefine the counselor's roles to emphasize outcomes and effects rather than functions and methods. Clients in each situation require counselors to make professional judgments about the most effective interventions in order to bring about improvements not only in the clients' behavior, but also in the environment in which the clients live. No one focus or limited conception of their role and no single strategy will enable counselors to be effective with the wide range of clients, client problems, and interests that they encounter in their varied settings.

Dr. Drapela has made a significant contribution to the emerging reconceptualization of counselor interventions and counselor opportunities by suggesting that it is important for the counselor to be involved in both consultation and supervision. He further suggests that the underlying psychodynamics involved in these two interventions are basically similar and that the difference between them lies in the length of the relationship (usually short for consultation and extended for supervision) and in the focus of the interpersonal interactions (the staff in consultation and the line in supervision). This conceptualization suggests that counselors can use their psychodiagnostic relationship building, psychometric understanding, and personal insight skills in a variety of individual and group situations. This book challenges us to think of ways that we may "give away" our skills and insights to the benefit of the populations that we work with either individually or in groups. Through consultation and supervision, we can help a variety of individuals and groups in numerous settings and situations to be more effective, thereby bringing about many of the ends and outcomes consistent with counseling but using different strategies and procedures.

This extension of the counselor role, or enhancement of the counselor role to include consultation and supervision, requires that all counselors who would transcend traditional modes of operation examine their own attitudes toward the new and heady role that he proposes. Clearly, many counselors may miss the dynamics and reassurance of previous direct counseling relationships, but if they can see and understand the positive benefits that will accrue to those who involve themselves in consultation and supervision, they will be more willing to give up a little of what they have done so well in the past in order to learn and involve themselves in new arenas where they may experience even greater rewards.

I am particularly pleased with the way Dr. Drapela has chosen to acquaint counselors with the variety of intervention strategies and methods that they might use. The time for dogmatic espousal of the merits of a single method for assisting our clients is past. Rather, we need skillful identification of client needs and customized interventions to suit both the person and the situation, in order to maximize the impact of our time and resources.

Historically, counseling has undergone a continuous struggle to expand the client populations that can be served and to improve the delivery of counseling services. In the ethos of the 1980s and 1990s, there is a new imperative to pay particular attention to our accountability and our commitment to do what we say we can and will do. There has always been a bit of the idealist and the dreamer in counselors; there is a belief in the capacity of persons to reach self-fulfillment through their own efforts and with the assistance of counselors. Experience has caused us to be less sure of how often such self-fulfillment can occur for an individual and of the role that we play in any individual's self-fulfillment. A book such as Dr. Drapela's, however, can be very helpful to all of us, expanding our armamentarium so that we may extend the populations we serve and enhance the quality of the services we provide. In the coming competitive struggle for those important social services we can provide, it will be said that counseling defined to include consultation and supervision is a service so vital and essential to society that it must be continued and supported in its continuing development. Those counselors who wish to be part of the future would do well to heed the scriptures of the future, which Dr. Drapela offers us. The writing in this case is not "on the wall"; it is in important documents such as Dr. Drapela's book. If we are to be a vital force for the future, we truly must learn it and act upon it.

Garry R. Walz

PREFACE

THIS book has been written for graduate students in counselor education programs and for practicing counselors who have had no course work in consultation and supervision as part of their professional training. The book is not meant for the training of specialists in the two professional fields, but for helping counseling practitioners gain a solid understanding of consultation and supervision theory and acquire needed skills and confidence to assume consulting or supervisory roles when circumstances demand it.

The distinctive feature of this volume is the systematic linkage of consultation and supervision within a unified conceptual framework. This approach is based on the generally accepted premises that the two helping functions require parallel skills, employ the same strategies, address similar issues, and have common goals. Consultation and supervision are additionally linked to counseling, thus constituting a helping triad that offers counselors a virtually unlimited range of opportunities for responding to people's needs.

The content of the book is based on, and documented by, current literature from the professional fields of counseling, school guidance, educational theory and practice, social psychology, social work, and organizational theory. The format of the book reflects my conviction that clarity and conciseness are desirable qualities of a textbook in themselves and are appreciated by students and instructors alike. For that reason, the narrative was kept brief and repetitions were avoided.

Titles of publications particularly useful for additional explanation or clarification of the issues discussed in the book were marked with an asterisk in the list of references following each chapter. They are recommended as supplementary readings and for further study in areas in which the reader wishes to attain greater expertise.

Graphical illustrations were used throughout the book for the benefit of visually oriented readers to clarify the narrative, to prevent ambiguity, and to lend a degree of concreteness to theoretical issues. To emphasize the logical and functional relatedness of counseling, consultation, and supervision, a matrix of helping processes, the Three-Dimensional Intervention Model, was developed. Its diagram serves as an overall framework for classifying all helping interventions discussed in the book. It is reproduced in most chapters with the perimeter of the respective helping intervention drawn in bold outline within the framework of the model.

V.J.D.

ACKNOWLEDGMENTS

I AM indebted to many persons who assisted me in this writing project. My graduate students with whom I shared parts of the manuscript gave me ample feedback during classroom discussions. Norma Caltagirone and Marian Martin read the entire manuscript and made editorial suggestions that improved its style and clarity. My colleague, William F. Benjamin reviewed the completed work and offered me the benefit of his judgment and professional critique. Garry Walz, professor of the University of Michigan and director of ERIC/CAPS Clearinghouse, wrote the Foreword.

I was also fortunate to receive effective technical support. My graduate assistant, Tammy Kimpland, was tireless in her daily cooperation through the crucial, final stage of the writing project, while Susan Allen typed the entire manuscript on the word processor and was always ready to make changes in the text. Mike Sadusky assumed responsibility for the final proofreading, and Joanne Sammis spent long hours preparing the subject index. Sections of the manuscripts were typed by Carolyn Hines, Lori Samuelson, and Kaji Cartwright.

Throughout the writing project, my wife, Gwen, gave me her loving support and was always willing to serve as a professional sounding board when I needed it most.

CONTENTS

THE COUNSELOR
AS CONSULTANT AND
SUPERVISOR

CHAPTER 1

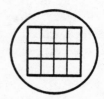

INTRODUCTION

NEW TRENDS IN THE WORK OF COUNSELORS

THE scope of counseling services has significantly grown during the past twenty years. Rapid social changes, altered lifestyles, and the profound impact of technology on the lives of individuals and families generated new problems in society. At the same time, the counselors' clientele has increased in numbers by members of population groups whose needs had been neglected in the past. As counseling programs grew in size and diversity, the work of counselors breached the perimeters of its traditional settings in educational institutions, vocational agencies, and mental health centers. In the process, counselors had to assume new helping roles of consultants and supervisors (or trainers) of other human services workers.

Consultation, in particular, has become a significant part of counselor functioning. This is true not only of school counselors, who regularly consult with teachers, parents of students, school psychologists, and social workers, but also of counselors in human services agencies, where interdisciplinary consultation is considered routine procedure. Many counselors also perform some supervisory work as part of their jobs, at least occasionally. Although not appointed to serve as supervisors, they assume supervisory roles when working with interns, practicum students, junior colleagues, or paraprofessionals. Are these shifts in counselor roles a reaction to outside pressures for an organizational realignment of services based on the criteria of accountability? Certainly to some degree. However, the fundamental reason for these shifts lies within the profession itself and is clearly linked to the current thrust among counselors toward change agentry.

Counselors as Change Agents

Since the 1960s, the American counseling profession has been in a soul-searching mood. Traditional assumptions were questioned and professional priorities reassessed. One of the issues discussed was the apparent inconsistency of the profession's emphasis on helping clients through counseling alone without paying sufficient attention to the cultural climate or organizational system in which clients live. Numerous counselors have pointed out that certain emotional problems of their clients have resulted from exposure to a pathogenic environment or to a dehumanizing system. Sarason (1971) and Walz and Benjamin (1977) assert that clients who remain within such settings cannot be adequately helped by counseling alone and that the solution of their problems lies in changing the environment rather than in helping clients adjust to it.

It may be overly pessimistic to term most existing institutions dehumanizing or dysfunctional. However, even in relatively healthy institutions, particularly in educational settings, there is need for ongoing change and renewal (Cook, 1972; Havelock, 1973). Change agentry does not detract from the ultimate aims of counseling — to help individuals develop into well-integrated persons who are self-acceptant, self-directive, and socially responsible. It is precisely for the purpose of attaining these aims more effectively that many counselors are shifting a major portion of their time and energy from individual and group counseling to changing the environment in which their clients live and work.

Change agentry is closely linked to consultation and supervision. Walz and Benjamin (1977, 1978) emphasize the major role that consultation plays in all innovation projects and point out that change agents need to acquire consultation skills for success in their work. Supervision, too, is involved, at least indirectly, in the process of social renewal. It is through supervision that proactive programs are promoted and high levels of staff enthusiasm are maintained. If counselors are to be actively involved in advancing institutional and social change, they need the leadership and support of competent and socially sensitive supervisors.

COUNSELING, CONSULTATION, AND SUPERVISION: DEFINITIONS AND DISTINCTIONS

Professional literature presents numerous examples of conceptual ambiguity and lack of differentiation when dealing with counseling, consultation, and supervision. For instance, Schmidt and Osborne (1981) point out that counseling and consulting require similar skills and techniques for helping people solve problems and make decisions. They conclude that "the theoretical and operational similarities between counseling and consulting are more prevalent than any differences between the two processes" (p. 171). Boyd (1978) emphasizes that consultation and supervision are closely interlinked and that virtually all supervisors use consultation as their principal approach. He promotes the concept of *consulting supervision*, and recommends the role of *consulting supervisor*. This functional linkage is also confirmed by McGreevy (1978) and by Moses and Hardin (1978), who comment on consultation and supervision, respectively. All three authors agree on a list of virtually identical skills that need to be mastered for proficiency in both fields.

We see, then, that although in theory recognized as distinct activities, counseling, consultation, and supervision are closely interrelated in practice. To form a clear understanding of their similarities and differences, it will be helpful to present and compare their definitions.

Counseling is defined as a dynamic process in which a professional counselor helps a client or a group of clients (1) develop greater self-awareness, (2) explore personal problems and make realistic plans for solving them within available alternatives, (3) overcome existing obstacles, (4) arrive at meaningful decisions, and (5) grow emotionally and socially. In counseling, clients receive *direct* assistance from the professional helper.

Consultation is also an intepersonal process; however, the assistance, which the consultant offers the consultee, is primarily for the benefit of a third party: the client. The consultant's assistance to the client (either an individual or a group) is *indirect*, by means of supporting the effort of the client's helper. In other respects, the consultation and the counseling processes are similar. Both cognitive and emotive approaches are involved, and attitudes and skills typical of counseling are equally useful in consultation. The special value of consultation lies in the combined efforts of consultant and consultee that result in a more effective assistance for the client.

Supervision, literally, is the process of overseeing and evaluating the activities of one or more workers for the purpose of assuring that envisioned goals are attained. In this context, counselor supervisors primarily focus on *indirect* assistance to clients who are consumers of the counseling services. Yet the humanistic tradition of counseling requires that the supervisory relationship be a genuine interpersonal process and that supervisors not overlook the personal needs of supervisees while promoting their professional enhancement. Thus, counselor supervision also contains *direct* assistance to the supervised counselors.

When we compare these definitions, we can conclude that the three professional activities have a common purpose of helping people in their problem-solving and developmental processes. The main differences lie in the methods of delivering this assistance. Figure 1-1 shows the relationship of counseling, consultation, and supervision in graphic form.

Supervision as a Helping Activity

Most people readily agree that counseling and consultation belong in the category of helping activities, but they may have their doubts as to the nature of supervision. To buttress the view that counselor supervision is a helping rather than a controlling activity, a brief explanation is in order.

The authoritarian supervisor or manager who projects the image of a privileged boss certainly is not on the endangered species list. However, that stereotype has been rejected as counter-

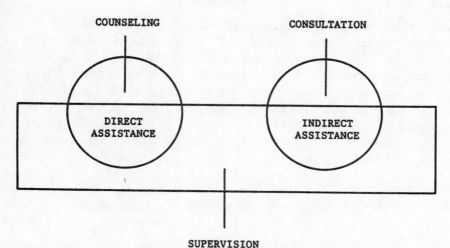

Figure 1-1. Similarities and Differences in Counseling, Consultation, and Supervision

productive by management theorists and by industry sources a-like. As early as two decades ago, Bennis (1966) asserted that "most rapidly blooming companies in the United States boast unusually democratic organizations" and that their executives and supervising personnel are attending human relation and organizational programs "to learn skills and attitudes which ten years ago would have been denounced as anarchic and revolutionary" (p. 18).* He concluded that the democratic management model was not merely an ideal to be sought but a necessary prerequisite "for survival under conditions of chronic change" (p. 19).*

What management in industrial and business organizations does primarily out of profit motivation, counselor supervisors should endeavor on the basis of their philosophical commitments. Since providing help to others is the highest priority of the coun-

*From *Beyond Bureaucracy: Essays on the Development and Evolution of Human Organizations* by W. Bennis. Copyright © 1966. Used with the permission of McGraw-Hill Book Co.

seling profession, the helping dimension should naturally permeate all processes of counselor supervision. Supervisors should realize that they are dealing with professional colleagues rather than "running programs." It is through their skill to actualize (rather than manipulate) the supervised counselors that successful supervisors promote high levels of motivation and work output. We shall see later that effective consultation and supervision models closely parallel well-established counseling strategies, not only in the human services area, but also in industrial and corporate settings.

THE PRESENT STATE OF PROFESSIONAL TRAINING IN CONSULTATION AND SUPERVISION

The Association for Counselor Education and Supervision (ACES) has mandated theoretical and practical training in consultation and supervision in all counselor education programs (ACES, 1973; 1978). However, thus far, this mandate has not been implemented in the majority of counselor education curricula.

Randolph (1980) complains that professional literature has generally failed to provide adequate recommendations on how consultation skills should be taught. The lack of specific course offerings in consultation is documented by Miles and Hummel (1979) who surveyed ninety-two graduate programs of counselor education. They found that less than one-third (32.5 percent) of the programs had courses in consultation, required as part of the curriculum at the master's level, and only 27.5 percent of them had such courses at the advanced graduate level. On a more positive note, the study found that some of the responding institutions were either preparing courses in consultation or were covering basic consultation processes in other curricular components.

As for course work in supervision, the current situation in counselor education programs is not satisfactory either. Boyd (1978) summarizes the results of several surveys on the educational background of persons holding supervisory positions in agencies, school systems, and in guidance units of state departments. He concludes that even those supervisors who hold advanced graduate degrees have received no specific preparation for their supervisory role. The majority of supervisors in agencies and state departments did not even complete a counseling practicum. It is assumed that they were promoted to their positions on the basis of earned academic degrees, successful counseling careers, and tenure within the system.

A Suggested Course Format

The preceding information dramatizes the need for an academic course that would help *all* counselors in training gain a clear understanding of consultation and supervision as a natural extension of the counseling function. Consultation and supervision processes closely parallel the counseling process, and the skills used in consultation and supervision are in reality modified counseling skills. In addition to the *logical* feasibility, there are also *pragmatic* reasons for presenting consultation and supervision in a unified didactic framework. Under the current fiscal conditions, it is more realistic to plan on adding one rather than two courses to an academic curriculum. The two neglected areas of counselor functioning will have a better chance of getting the attention they deserve if the subject matter is presented in an integrated form and if the course of study is not overly lengthy.

The proposed didactic format, based on the organizational structure and content of this book, is meant for a graduate course in counselor education. However, with minor adjustments it can also be used for adding new learning experiences to existing courses or for creating in-service training programs. The theoretical study should always be supplemented by practicum or field experiences under professional supervision by the course instructor or by an experienced consultant or supervisor.

ORGANIZATION OF THE BOOK

Section I provides the theoretical framework for understanding the nature of counseling, consultation, and supervision. It focuses on those elements that are common to the three professional functions. Particular attention is given to the following issues:

1. The classification of a counselor's helping interventions within a unified framework
2. The personality profile typical of effective helpers, particularly consultants and supervisors
3. The processes and stages of consultation and supervision
4. The helping strategies used on consultation and supervision

Section II applies the theoretical insights to helping interventions for the benefit of individuals and groups and discusses —

1. Consultation with professionals, primarily teachers and administrators, and parents of students
2. Supervision of counselors in training
3. Supervision of counseling practitioners

Section III explores the use of consultative approaches in change agentry, particularly for the following purposes:

1. Promoting organizational development in institutions
2. Fostering social change in the community through outreach programs
3. Evaluating the effectiveness of change agentry projects in institutions and in the community

SUMMARY

1. As the scope of counseling services expanded in past years, consultation and supervision gained increased importance in counselor functioning.

2. Consultation and supervision are closely linked to the current thrust of the counseling profession toward change agentry, an attempt at restructuring the environment in which people live and work.

3. To help counselors clarify the relationship of the various helping functions in their professional repertory, the definitions of counseling, consultation, and supervision have been presented. Special emphasis has been placed on identifying counselor supervision as a helping rather than controlling activity.

4. The current state of professional training in consultation and supervision is not satisfactory. Recent studies indicate that contrary to a mandate by ACES, most counselor education programs offer no course work in consultation and supervision.

5. To remedy this void in counselor education, a course that would integrate the study of consultation and supervision conceptually and operationally has been recommended. The format of the course could be based on the structure and content of this volume.

REFERENCES

*ACES: *Standards for the Preparation of Counselors and Other Personnel Services Specialists.* Washington, ACES, 1973 (mimeographed).

ACES: Guidelines for doctoral preparation in counselor education. *Counselor Education and Supervision, 17*:163-166, 1978.

Bennis, W.: *Beyond Bureaucracy: Essays on the Development and Evolution of Human Organizations.* New York, McGraw-Hill, 1966.

Boyd, J.D.: *Counselor Supervision: Approaches, Preparation, Practices.* Muncie, IN, Accelerated Development, 1978.

Cook, D.R.: The change agent counselor: A conceptual context. *The School Counselor, 20*:9-15, 1972.

Havelock, R.G.: *The Change Agent's Guide to Innovation in Education.* Englewood Cliffs, NJ, Educational Technology Publications, 1973.

*McGreevy, C.P.: Training consultants: Issues and approaches. *Personnel and Guidance Journal, 56*:432-435, 1978.

*Miles, J.H., and Hummel, D.L.: Consultant training in counselor education programs. *Counselor Education and Supervision, 19*:49-53, 1979.

Moses, H.A., and Hardin, J.T.: A relationship approach to counselor supervision in agency settings. In Boyd, J. (Ed.): *Counselor Supervision: Approaches, Preparation, Practices.* Muncie, IN, Accelerated Development, 1978, pp. 441-480.

Randolph, D.: Teaching consultation for mental health and educational settings. *Counselor Education and Supervision, 20*:117-124, 1980.

Sarason, S.B.: *The Culture of the School and the Problem of Change.* Boston, Allyn and Bacon, 1971.

*Schmidt, J.J., and Osborne, W.L.: Counseling and consulting: Separate processes or the same? *Personnel and Guidance Journal, 60*:168-171, 1981.

Walz, G.R., and Benjamin, L.: *On Becoming a Change Agent.* Ann Arbor, MI, ERIC/CAPS Clearinghouse, 1977.

Walz, G.R., and Benjamin, L.: A change agent strategy for counselors functioning as consultants. *Personnel and Guidance Journal, 56*:331-334, 1978.

---

*Recommended readings

Section I
THEORETICAL FOUNDATIONS OF COUNSELING, CONSULTATION, AND SUPERVISION

SECTION I of this volume contains the theoretical foundations that underlie counseling, consultation, and supervision: their rationale, methodology, and developmental patterns. Chapter 2 presents a theoretical framework for understanding and classifying all helping processes in terms of targets of intervention, issues to be addressed, and strategies to be used.

Chapter 3 explores the profile of helping professionals, including their personal traits and values, their professional attitudes and skills, and their experiential background. Chapter 4 is devoted to the processes and stages of consultation and supervision. Particular attention is given to the meaning of the process dimension versus the product or content dimensions. Chapter 5 analyzes the three basic helping strategies used in consultation and supervision and points to their close relationship with counseling strategies. It also emphasizes the need for each helping professional to develop a helping style that would reflect his or her life experiences, personal philosophy and values, and professional orientation.

CHAPTER 2

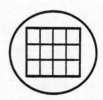

A CONCEPTUAL FRAMEWORK

A S their roles expand, many counselors are not certain in which direction to move and how to prioritize their efforts. They understand the short-term goals of their helping interventions but wonder about the overall configuration of the new strategies. They are improvising and responding to immediate needs rather than planning long-range, proactive programs.

To remedy this lack of direction among counselors, several useful efforts have been made at providing a basic topography, a conceptual road map, for the expanding territory of human services. Two of the more important examples of such efforts are discussed below.

THE CUBE

Early in the past decade, Morrill, Oetting, and Hurst (1974) noted that no systematic attempts have been made at offering a meaningful description of the new dimensions of counselor functioning that involved outreach programs, the use of paraprofessionals, consultation services, etc. They noted that a descriptive model for new counselor roles was needed along with a taxonomy of helping interventions that would link them into an organic system. They proposed a three-dimensional matrix, which they called the Cube, shown in Figure 2-1.* As the three axes intersect at various levels, they pinpoint the nature of numerous interventions in terms of (a) targets, (b) purposes, and (c) methods.

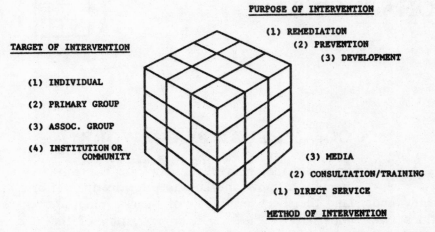

PURPOSE OF INTERVENTION

(1) REMEDIATION
(2) PREVENTION
(3) DEVELOPMENT

TARGET OF INTERVENTION

(1) INDIVIDUAL
(2) PRIMARY GROUP
(3) ASSOC. GROUP
(4) INSTITUTION OR COMMUNITY

(3) MEDIA
(2) CONSULTATION/TRAINING
(1) DIRECT SERVICE

METHOD OF INTERVENTION

Figure 2-1. The Cube. Modified from W.H. Morrill, E.R. Oetting, and J.C. Hurst, Dimensions of counselor functioning, *Personnel and Guidance Journal,* 52:354-359. Reprinted by permission. Copyright © 1974 held by Morrill, Oetting, and Hurst.

Targets of Interventions

The targets of interventions are listed as follows:

1. *Individuals,* typically approached on a one-to-one basis or within a small group
2. *Primary Groups* that emerge naturally and exert a strong influence on the behavior of individuals, e.g. the family and close friends
3. *Associational Groups* that do not emerge naturally but are formed either by choice or by chance associations as a result of similar interests and needs of members, e.g. clubs, school units, college students staying on the same floor of a residence hall, and chapters of professional associations

---

*A slightly modified model of the Cube has been developed by the authors for work with students, particularly at the college level (Morrill, Hurst, and Oetting, 1980).

4. *Institutions or the Community* that are broader than associational groups and thus provide fewer opportunities for personal interaction of members, e.g. schools, neighborhoods, and religious organizations

Purposes of Interventions

The purposes of interventions are perceived in terms of –

1. *Remediation* that leads to the elimination of an existing problem
2. *Prevention* that anticipates and avoids future problems, provides people with needed skills, and promotes environmental changes that prevent problems, e.g. programs that help high school graduates transfer to college with minimal trauma
3. *Development*, i.e. proactive efforts that foster growth and social maturation of youngsters, such as informal rap sessions or other group projects

Methods of Interventions

The authors of the Cube consider the methods dimension important for understanding the *how* of any given intervention, i.e. the way in which the intervention is delivered to the target population. They recognize three kinds of approaches:

1. *Direct Service*: the typical delivery of assistance through counseling on a one-to-one basis or through group work; this approach has proven to be effective but it has certain limitations, such as the high cost of service delivery, the inability to reach all who need help, etc.
2. *Consultation and Training* of allied professionals and paraprofessionals: the range of existing counseling resources is expanded, and the impact of helping interventions may be enhanced since some population groups relate to paraprofessionals better than to professionals.
3. *Media*: involving a wide variety of hardware and software in the computer area, television programming, audio and video teaching aids, the press, etc.

The authors point out that such a conceptual framework not only helps counselors understand the variety of approaches available to them but also "provides a point of departure, a stimulus for creative thinking about alternative interventions" (Morrill, Oetting, and Hurst, 1974, p. 359).

The main value of the Cube is in the clarity of distinctions it provides: (1) between counseling and consultation or training, (2) among purposes of interventions, and (3) among categories of consumers of help. Its major limitation lies in the absence of methodological considerations. The various therapeutic strategies that can be used in the course of helping interventions have been extensively covered by the theoretical model that will be discussed next.

THE CONSULCUBE^{T.M.}

This three-dimensional matrix has been designed by Blake and Mouton (1976) to clarify various consultation behaviors. However, consultation is interpreted in the broadest sense and includes "all kinds of professional interventions" (Goodstein, 1978, p. 29). The three dimensions used in the Consulcube are (1) kinds of interventions, (2) focal issues of interventions, and (3) units of change.

The Cube and Consulcube have only one dimension in common: the consumers of helping interventions, termed *targets* or *units of change*, respectively. The other two dimensions are quite unrelated in the two models.

Blake and Mouton (1976) base their approach on the premise that all behavior of individuals and groups is cyclical in nature and resistant to change. Therefore, they consider all consulting interventions to be attempts at breaking these cyclical behavior patterns. In the authors' view, cycle breaking is the common denominator of consulting activities, no matter who the consultee may be — an individual, a group, or a large client system. Emphasis is placed on the various cycle-breaking strategies and on the central issues that must be addressed. The Consulcube is depicted in Figure 2-2.

Kinds of Interventions

This dimension is of major importance, for the same kind of intervention may be used across the entire perimeter of consultation in dealing with a variety of consultees and focusing on a variety of problems. Specifically, the kinds of interventions are —

1. *Acceptant*: an approach parallel to the attitude applied in person-centered counseling
2. *Catalytic*: assisting the consultee in reinterpreting his or her assessment of the existing situation
3. *Confrontation*: challenging the consultee's basic thinking processes, which may have distorted the perceived reality because of value-laden premises
4. *Prescriptive*: a directive approach that formulates the solution of the problem for the consultee
5. *Theories and Principles*: a teaching approach that helps the consultee absorb new knowledge on the basis of which he or she can diagnose and remedy existing problems*

The authors point out that these kinds of interventions may be applied in pure form or as a mixture of approaches and that the majority of consultants develop a personal style of intervention that they rely on, at times to an excessive degree.

Focal Issues for Interventions

The four focal issues listed are interdependent. When a change is occurring in one, the others are affected simultaneously, or will be affected eventually. For instance, an appropriate adjustment of professional norms and standards will positively affect the level of staff morale and the degree of cohesion among staff members.

Specifically, the focal issues are —

1. *Power/Authority* as used in the consultee's setting
2. *Morale/Cohesion* within the group addressed by the consultation process
3. *Norms/Standards* of behavior and of occupational activities

---

*In a revised edition of their book, Blake and Mouton (1983) have reversed the order of interventions.

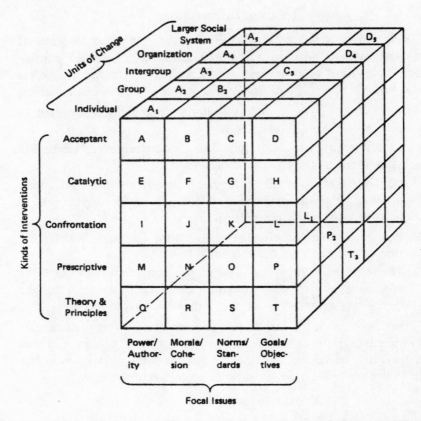

Figure 2-2. The Consulcube[TM]. Reprinted from *Consultation* by Robert R. Blake and Jane S. Mouton. Copyright © 1976 by Scientific Methods Inc., by permission of Addison-Wesley Publishing Co., Reading, MA.

4. *Goals/Objectives* of individual or team effort, of institutions, or specific programs

There is a relationship between the focal issue in a problem situation and the kind of intervention that is most useful in dealing with it. The authors feel that the intensity of an issue often dictates a particular intervention. For instance, they consider it impractical to apply theory and principles when the intensity of an issue is either too high or too low. A fanatical person or a disinterested individual will not respond to theory but rather to other kinds of interventions, e.g. catalysis and confrontation. It follows that an accurate identification of the focal issue is the chief prerequisite for success in consulting work.

Units of Change

As mentioned earlier, this dimension is identical with the target of intervention dimension of the Cube. There are only minor differences between the two. Blake and Mouton (1975) do not list primary and associational groups separately, but they add the *intergroup* category that denotes the relationship between two units, e.g. divisions or departments.

The chief value of the Consulcube lies in its virtually universal applicability, which is based on the five interventions available to consultants, no matter who they may be — psychologists, clergymen, parents, or teachers. Its basic limitation, particularly for didactic use, is the lack of a clear taxonomy of helping functions. Specifically, no distinction is made between helping functions that involve direct service and indirect service. All of them, ranging from personal counseling and treatment of phobias to organizational renewal and control of street violence, are dealt with together.

THE THREE-DIMENSIONAL INTERVENTION MODEL

The two theoretical models discussed above are useful for classifying a wide variety of professional interventions. However, neither model is suitable for the combined study of counseling, consultation, and supervision. To facilitate understanding of the three professional functions in terms of their mutual relationships, I am presenting here my own matrix, the Three-Dimensional Intervention Model, which is geared to the specific objectives of this volume.

The three dimensions of the matrix run parallel to those of the Consulcube, but the categories within each dimension are different. While the structure of the Consulcube is complex, containing 100 cells, the structure of the model proposed here is relatively simple, having only forty-eight cells. Yet, all principal interventions that a counselor typically carries out within the perimeters of counseling, consultation, and supervision are covered.

Every intervention is identified in terms of (1) the target of intervention, i.e. persons or groups that are assisted (Arabic numerals); (2) the issue that needs to be addressed for resolving a problem or promoting growth (capital letters); and (3) the strategy that the helper uses (Roman numerals). Every intervention can be expressed in code (e.g. 1-A-I), which will be explained later in this chapter. A graphic interpretation of the three-dimensional intervention Model in Figure 2-3 will add clarity to the narrative description of the three dimensions used in the model.

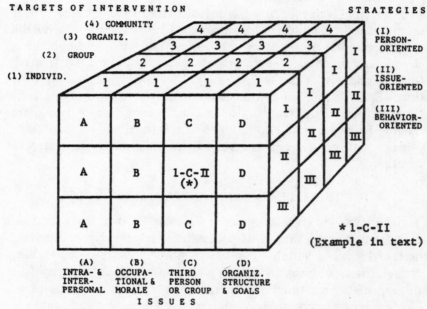

Figure 2-3. The Three-Dimensional Intervention Model.

First Dimension: Targets of Intervention

1. *Individuals*: professionals and nonprofessionals of any background, i.e. clients, consultees, and supervisees
2. *Groups*: both primary groups (e.g. families and neighbor-

hoods) and associational groups (e.g. clubs) formed by choice or out of necessity

3. *Organizations*: units of persons organized for a specific purpose and operating under a set of rules, e.g. schools, agencies, school districts, scientific institutions, and corporate and industrial systems

4. *Community*: a large number of persons who, because of geographical proximity or mutual interests, belong to a major political subdivision, such as a city, county, or state, to an ethnic population group, or to a large interest group, such as a national federation

Second Dimension: Issues to Be Addressed

A. *Intrapersonal and Interpersonal*: any concerns or problems of a personal or social nature that are not job-related

B. *Occupational Concerns, Morale*: concerns related to a person's occupation, e.g. actual or perceived quality of performance, job satisfaction, professional identity, and team cohesion

C. *Third Person or Group*: third-party issues concerning an individual or a group, e.g. behavior problems of students — a third party — that compel a teacher to seek assistance through consultation

D. *Organizational Structure and Goals*: problems that are inherent to an organizational structure, e.g. lack of communication, organizational rigidity, and dehumanizing procedures

Third Dimension: Strategies of Intervention

I. *Person-Oriented Strategy (Subjective, Affective)*: approaches that focus on the inner world of the person as experienced by the person

II. *Issue-Oriented Strategy (Objective, Cognitive)*: data-based, analytical methods for problem solving

III. *Behavior-Oriented Strategy (Behavioral Methodology)*: reinforcement techniques, behavior modification, social modeling, etc.

Interventions Expressed in Code

As mentioned earlier, any of the forty-eight cells of this three-dimensional matrix refers to a specific intervention that can be expressed in code. For instance, code 1-C-II refers to an intervention by which an *individual* is assisted to deal with a *third-party problem* and in which the helper uses the *issue-oriented strategy*:

Target of Intervention: 1
Issue to be Addressed: C
Strategy of Intervention: II

The code of this intervention can be found in its appropriate cell in Figure 2-3. Another example: Code 3-B-III refers to a helping intervention on behalf of an organization (target 3) dealing with occupational problems or personnel morale (issue B) in which behavioral approaches (strategy III) are used.

PERIMETERS OF PROFESSIONAL FUNCTIONS

On the basis of the Three-Dimensional Intervention Model, it is relatively simple to identify the perimeters of counseling, consultation, and supervision.

Perimeter of Counseling

Since counseling is done on a one-to-one basis or in groups, only two intervention targets, individuals (1) and groups (2) are appropriate. The issues addressed in counseling are primarily intrapersonal and interpersonal (A) but occupational issues (B) may also be addressed. The perimeter of counseling is shown in Figure 2-4.

The counseling process may at times touch upon third-party or organizational issues (C and D), such as problems of the client's relatives or the administrative structure of the client's work setting. To the extent that these issues directly affect the client's intrapersonal domain, they become part of the counseling perimeter.

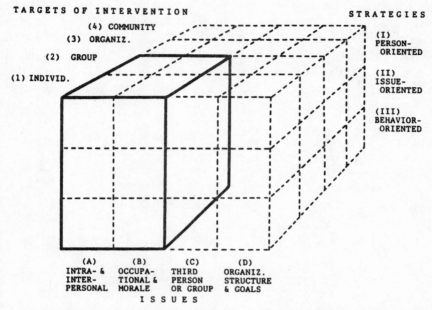

TARGETS OF INTERVENTION

(4) COMMUNITY
(3) ORGANIZ.
(2) GROUP
(1) INDIVID.

STRATEGIES

(I)
PERSON-
ORIENTED

(II)
ISSUE-
ORIENTED

(III)
BEHAVIOR-
ORIENTED

(A)
INTRA- &
INTER-
PERSONAL

(B)
OCCUPA-
TIONAL &
MORALE

(C)
THIRD
PERSON
OR GROUP

(D)
ORGANIZ.
STRUCTURE
& GOALS

I S S U E S

Figure 2-4. Perimeter of Counseling (Solid Lines) within the Three-Dimensional Intervention Model (Dotted Lines).

Overlap of Counseling and Consultation

The true gray area between counseling and consultation is issue B, occupational concerns and morale, which is typically absorbed by one or the other perimeter, depending on the issue with which it is linked. If occupational concerns are linked with an individual's intrapersonal problems (issue A), they fall in the perimeter of counseling. This may be the case when job-related tensions are at the root of emotional problems of a client who receives counseling. Conversely, if occupational issues are linked with the problem of a third party (issue C), they fall in the perimeter of consultation. This may be the case when a teacher's lack of occupational skills is the major cause of student misbehavior (third-party problem) that is being dealt with through consultation.

Figure 2-5 indicates the area of overlap of counseling and consultation. To expand on the above example, a teacher who is unable to control her class jeopardizes both her self-concept and the welfare of her students. Counseling will help her deal with her feelings. Consultation will aid her in upgrading her professional skills for the benefit of the students — a third party — and also for her own benefit.

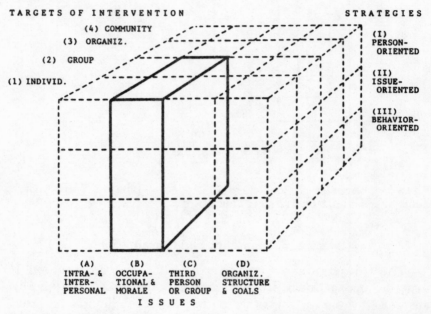

Figure 2-5. Area of Overlap of Counseling and Consultation (Solid Lines) within the Three-Dimensional Intervention Model (Dotted Lines).

Perimeter of Consultation

This perimeter covers the major portion of the Three-Dimensional Intervention Model. It takes in all targets of intervention. When dealing with individuals and groups (targets 1 and 2), consultation addresses issues B, C, and D. When dealing with organizations or the community (targets 3 and 4), consultation primarily focuses on issues B, C, and D, but also impacts the intrapersonal and interpersonal functioning of people (issue A) who are members of an organization or of the community. In consultation, all strategies (I, II, and III) are used.

Figure 2-6 dramatizes the broad range of helping interventions that becomes available to counselors who are willing to use the consultation approach. The various consultation modalities available to counselors will be explained in subsequent chapters.

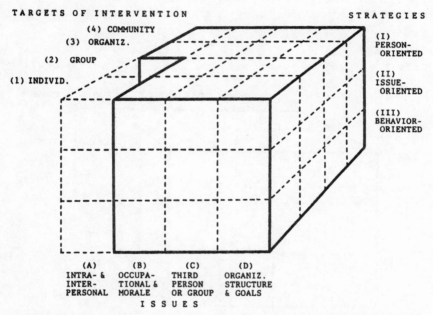

Figure 2-6. Perimeter of Consultation (Solid Lines) within the Three-Dimensional Intervention Model (Dotted Lines).

Perimeter of Supervisory Functions

As will be explained later, supervision makes extensive use of consultation, often in combination with counseling. It is accurate to state that supervision, particularly supervision of counselors in training, is either consultation or counseling. As is shown in Figure 2-7, the boundaries of supervision coincide with the boundaries of individual and group counseling and consultation.

By its nature, supervision is functionally restricted to intervention targets 1 and 2 (individuals and groups), i.e. to counselors, allied professionals, and paraprofessionals for whose performance the supervisor is responsible. However, within this perimeter, the supervisor can apply a variety of approaches (I, II, and III). At times, supervision deals with problems of the counselor's clients or with the organizational structure of the counselor's work setting (issues C and D). At other times, supervision focuses on personal or professional issues (A and B) of the supervised counselors.

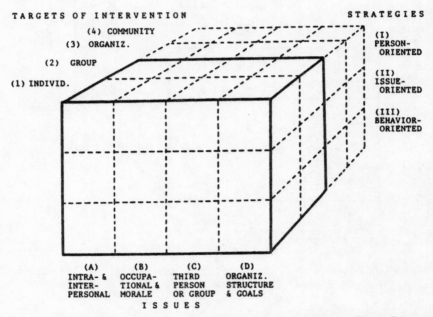

Figure 2-7. Perimeter of Supervision (Solid Lines) within the Three-Dimensional Intervention Model (Dotted Lines).

Understanding the nature and mutual relationship of the principal helping functions is of major importance for counseling practitioners. It helps them see the entire field of human services and differentiate the various roles they have to assume in it. It increases their sense of purpose and places their personal contribution to the profession into sharper focus. It also facilitates the coordination and integration of helping efforts carried out by teams of professionals — among them, counselors and educators — in the community.

SUMMARY

1. As the scope of helping interventions widens, counselors are in need of a conceptual framework that would shed new light on their expanding professional territory.

2. One example of such conceptual framework is the Cube developed by Morrill, Oetting, and Hurst (1974). It identifies counselor interventions in terms of target, purpose, and method.

3. Another conceptual model, the Consulcube, conceived by Blake and Mouton (1976), limits its focus to the area of consultation, although consultation is perceived in broad terms. The dimensions used in that model are kinds of interventions, focal issues for interventions, and units of change.

4. For the specific purpose of combining the study of counseling, consultation, and supervision into a single educational experience, the author of this volume is presenting his own Three-Dimensional Intervention Model. He suggests three dimensions — the targets of helping interventions, the issues, and the strategies — for describing all forty-eight interventions contained in the matrix. Every intervention can be expressed in code.

5. The perimeters of counseling, consulting, and supervision are identified through a topographic analysis of the cube-like structure of the model.

REFERENCES

*Blake, R.R., and Mouton, J.S.: *Consultation.* Reading, MA, Addison-Wesley, 1976.

Blake, R.R., and Mouton, J.S.: *Consultation: A Handbook for Individual and Organization Development.* Reading, MA, Addison-Wesley, 1983.

---

*Recommended reading

Goodstein, L.D.: *Consulting with Human Service Systems.* Reading, MA, Addison-Wesley, 1978.

*Morrill, W.H., Hurst, J.C., and Oetting, E.R.: *Dimensions of Intervention for Student Development.* New York, Wiley, 1980.

*Morrill, W.H., Oetting, E.R., and Hurst, J.C.: Dimensions of counselor functioning. *Personnel and Guidance Journal, 52*:354-359, 1974.

---

*Recommended readings

CHAPTER 3

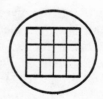

THE HELPING PROFESSIONAL

E FFECTIVE consultants and supervisors are not necessarily charismatic individuals. However, all of them have been endowed with certain personality traits, interest in and sensitivity to people, which are vital prerequisites for successful theoretical training and for development of professional maturity. Not all music lovers will become successful opera singers, no matter how ambitious their efforts. They need a basic aptitude to succeed as performers in the field of music. Similarly, not all people interested in human behavior or social structures have the natural prerequisites for effective work in the helping professions.

Successful helping professionals may differ from each other in many ways but they match a basic profile that is a combination of (1) personal traits and values, (2) professional attitudes and skills, and (3) adequate work experiences. This chapter presents an analysis of the profile.

PERSONAL TRAITS AND VALUES

Members of the counseling profession know that their principal therapeutic tool is their own personality. To be effective, they have to serve as role models for the people whom they assist in their growth process. They need to be authentic human beings with well-integrated, therapeutic personalities and with caring attitudes. The personality profile of effective helpers can be described in the following terms.

Self-Awareness

This involves being attuned to the full range of experiences and having a clear understanding of one's priorities and long-term goals. Effective helpers are responsive to their needs, comfortable with their feelings (Rogers, 1951), and aware of their motivation (Adler, 1930). In the process of maturing, they have developed an optimistic outlook on life, a high degree of self-objectivity, and a sense of humor (Allport, 1961). These qualities help them cope with the problems of life.

Self-Acceptance

Self-acceptance is the outgrowth of a positive self-concept. Helping professionals accept themselves the way they are, with their strengths and abilities but also with their limitations and weaknesses (Combs and Snygg, 1959). They accustom themselves to those limitations that are unavoidable and permanent, and they patiently counteract temporary limitations and avoidable weaknesses.

Self-accepting persons do not overly depend on the approval of others for maintaining their self-esteem; however, they appreciate the goodwill and friendship shown to them. They are simultaneously self-confident and humble, and they are aware of their acquired knowledge and skills but also realize how much more there is to be mastered in theoretical knowledge and in clinical proficiency.

Maturity

Effective helpers have formed a sense of identity (Erikson, 1968), a meaning in their lives (Frankl, 1970), and realistic expectations for the future. When not measuring up to their own expectations, they are able to forgive themselves and try anew. They stimulate similar attitudes when dealing with others. Unattractive personality traits and behavioral failings of individuals are perceived as elements of the human fabric common to all people.

Maturity is also reflected in the assessment of new ideas and trends, which are evaluated according to valid standards rather than in terms of public acclaim. While rejecting fads, mature people are open-minded to new and unconventional approaches. When others insist that the established way of doing things is the best way, or when warnings are sounded against unconventional methods and innovative processes, mature persons challenge such stagnant positions.

Adequate Intelligence

To be successful, helping professionals have to possess a healthy combination of intellectual ability and motivation. Grasping complex patterns of human behavior and applying general principles to concrete situations require intelligence in any professional field. Counselors know from experience that understanding individual and group dynamics, assessing the nature and severity of a problem, and using appropriate communication skills are no easy tasks. It should be stated here that intellectual ability is not incompatible with personal warmth, sensitivity, and caring attitudes. The occasionally implied dichotomy of insensitive intellectualism and of warm-hearted intellectual mediocrity is not supported by evidence.

Decisiveness and Concreteness

These two traits, necessary in any helping intervention, are of particular significance for consultants and supervisors. This does not mean that consultants or supervisors should be autocratic and inflexible or impose their solutions on others. However, while working toward the solution of a problem, they have to promote concreteness of input and planning, and once a decision has been made, they have to press for implementation. Concreteness is also needed for translating one's knowledge into language clearly understood by nonprofessionals and into practical applications that are operationally sound.

Although there is need for flexibility in exploring alternatives, there is equal need for persistence in implementing realistic objectives. Consultants and supervisors must be resourceful when trying to overcome deadlocks and willing to take calculated risks when facing ethical dilemmas.

Concern for People

Most counselors know that unless they are strongly people-oriented, they cannot succeed in their jobs. Persons who place a high value on material rewards alone will find little satisfaction in the field of human services. The value orientation of effective helpers reflects a variety of altruistic and humanistic attitudes: interest in the inner world of people, respect and caring for people as individuals and members of groups, relating to people with warmth, and offering encouragement and assistance.

Traditionally, the primary commitment of helping professionals in our society has been to individuals — clients, consultees, and supervisees — rather than to the employing institution. This is a valid principle, consistent with the humanistic tradition of the counseling profession, as long as one realizes that the enhancement of the individual and the progress of society are interrelated.

Ideally, there should be no conflict between the need satisfaction of the individual and the organizational goals of the institution in which the person operates. If such a conflict emerges, it is either because individuals have unreasonable demands or because the institution is oppressive. It is up to those of us who act as consultants or supervisors to make every effort for establishing and maintaining a healthy balance between the legitimate needs of the individual and the aims of the institution.

Actualizing Behavior

In his book, *Man, the Manipulator*, Shostrom (1967) summarizes the typical personality traits and values of effective helping professionals. He presents the contrast of actualizing and manipulating behavior. Among the traits of an actualizor (the ideal helper) are honesty, authenticity, awareness, freedom, spontaneity, and trust. These are in sharp contrast with traits of manipulative persons, such as deception, boredom, control, and cynicism. Dinkmeyer and Carlson (1973) have a parallel perception of helping professionals, whom they call "facilitators of human potential." Another useful description of the typical helping personality has been provided by Combs, Avila, and Purkey (1971).

PROFESSIONAL ATTITUDES AND SKILLS

Every professional endeavor has to be built on a theoretical basis with a set of philosophical premises and ethical standards. The belief of Kurt Lewin that nothing is as practical as a good theory should be recalled here. A person's professional work always reflects his or her theoretical orientation, philosophical learning, and ethical commitment. On the other hand, if the profession is to have a concrete impact on society, skills, techniques, and applied strategies must also be given appropriate recognition.

Elements of Professionalism

In the view of Lippitt and Lippitt (1978), professionalism is characterized by the following elements that constitute a pattern:

1. Acquisition of adequate knowledge of theory in the professional field
2. Ability to translate professional theory into effective helping processes
3. Determination to put the interests of the consumer of service ahead of personal or own-group interest
4. Insistence on high standards of professional service to clients
5. Consistent professional behavior at all times*

The first and second item of this list refer to the theoretical knowledge and expertise the professional is expected to possess. The other items are related to professional ethics. Briefly stated, professionalism is the combination of two factors: full qualification (competence) and ethical integrity. Let us examine these two factors in some detail.

Full Qualification (Competence)

Professional counselors have to earn at least a master's degree, which involves extensive theoretical study and practicum or field experiences. To be effective consultants and supervisors, they may need additional training, depending on their educational back-

---

*Adapted from: G.L. Lippitt and R. Lippitt, *The Consulting Process in Action*. San Diego, CA, University Associates, 1978. Used with permission.

ground. Whereas counselors help clients, consultants and supervisors assist both fellow professionals and, indirectly, their clients. This additional responsibility is reason enough for higher levels of competence.

To help counseling practitioners acquire adequate levels of competence for success in consultation and supervision is, of course, the aim of this volume, and the relevant information will be presented in subsequent chapters. However, it should be added here that competence needs to be matched by initiative and creativity. At this stage, consultants and supervisors have to be willing to address new areas of human concerns and initiate untested, proactive helping programs as part of their professional mandate.

Ethical Integrity

Ethical integrity is a necessary condition for long-term success in any professional endeavor. This is especially true in the helping professions. Unless the client can fully trust the counselor, little or no therapeutic change will occur in his or her behavior. This also applies to the field of consultation and supervision. The following list of basic prerequisites for a relationship of trust between helper and helpee has been abstracted from the ethical standards of the American Personnel and Guidance Association (APGA, 1981):

- *Commitment.* The helping professional should strive continuously for improving professional practices. "Professional growth is continuous. . .and is exemplified by the development of a philosophy that explains why and how a member functions in the helping relationship" (Section A, 1).
- *Responsibility.* The helping professional "has a responsibility both to the individual who is served and to the institution within which the service is performed to maintain high standards of professional conduct" (Section A, 2).
- *Truth in Stating One's Qualifications.* The helping professional "neither claims nor implies professional qualifications exceeding those possessed and is responsible for correcting any misrepresentations of these qualifications by others" (Section A, 4). This concern is currently given attention in legislative circles throughout the nation. Several states have

already passed licensure laws for counselors and other helping professionals.

Welfare of Client. The client, consultee, or supervisee must receive primary consideration by the helping professional who is obligated "to respect the integrity and promote the welfare of the client(s), whether the client(s) is (are) assisted individually or in a group relationship" (Section B, 1). To safeguard consultees' and supervisees' welfare, helping professionals must promote self-direction in them rather than dependency.

- *Respect for the Client's Values.* Values cannot be separated from the helping relationship. Values which are universal, e.g. respect for the person, freedom of choice, truthfulness, etc., are therapeutic in themselves and should be promoted. However, helping professionals must avoid imposing their personal values on clients. Brammer (1979) warns helpers to resist the often unexpected feeling of power over helpees that may lead to controlling helpees' behavior.

- *Confidentiality.* All helping relationships require a degree of confidentiality. In consultation and supervision the range of confidentiality requirements may differ from counseling. However, all confidential information must always be treated as such, unless the originator of the information authorizes the professional to divulge it.

Lippitt and Lippitt (1978) make an interesting observation about the need for selective integration of ethical standards from various sources. Specifically, they recommend the blending of scientific ethics and humanistic ethics into what they call *scientific humanism.* Since forming one's value system is a highly personal matter, most helping professionals will use their own preferences based on cultural background and life experiences to guide them in choosing their values.

Professional Skills

Counseling Skills

This book is written for counselors in training and for practitioners who have completed their professional education. Thus, it would seem superfluous to discuss here the wide range of counseling skills that are to be used in consultation and supervision. References to particular skills will be made in subsequent chapters. Readers who wish to review counseling skills are referred to the book, *The Helping Relationship: Process and Skills,* by Lawrence M. Brammer (1979), from which I summarize the following skills inventory:

- *Listening Skills.* Noting verbal and nonverbal clues, paraphrasing and clarifying messages, and determining the accuracy of understanding
- *Leading Skills.* Direct and indirect leading, encouraging discussion, focusing and counteracting confusion, and questioning
- *Reflecting Skills.* Reflecting feelings and experience, and repeating ideas and paraphrasing them for emphasis
- *Summarizing Skills.* Tying themes together
- *Confronting Skills.* Recognizing and describing feelings in helper and helpee, promoting self-confrontation, tapping obscure feelings, and helping loosen feelings
- *Interpreting Skills.* Facilitating awareness and symbolizing ideas and feelings
- *Informing Skills.* Advice giving, offering suggestions based on experience, and presenting valid and accurate information*

Consultation Skills

Lippitt and Lippitt (1978) have compiled responses received from thirty-two consultants as to skills considered necessary for consultation. Their summary is presented here in condensed form:

- *Communication Skills.* Observing, listening, and reporting
- *Teaching and Persuading Skills.* Imparting new ideas and designing instructional experiences for growth and development

---

*Lawrence M. Brammer, *The Helping Relationship,* 2nd ed., © 1979, pp. 67-68. Adapted by permission of Prentice-Hall, Inc., Englewood Cliffs, NJ.

- *Counseling Skills.* Helping others to make good choices
- *Relationship Skills.* Ability to form trustful relationships and sensitivity to the feelings of people
- *Group Work Skills.* Ability to work with groups in planning and implementing change
- *Selectivity Skills.* Ability to use various interventions and to decide which intervention is most suitable in any given situation
- *Survey Skills.* Ability to gather various types of data
- *Diagnostic Skills.* Ability to identify problems of individuals and systems
- *Flexibility Skills.* Ability to deal with a variety of situations
- *Problem-Solving Skills.* Ability to use problem-solving techniques and to help others solve their problems*

Quinn (1980) offers suggestions as to how to use many of these consultation skills when working with teachers, administrators, and parents in school settings.

Supervision Skills

Skills necessary for supervision include all counseling and consulting skills (many of which overlap) and the following:

- *Modeling and Motivational Skills.* Acting as role model for trainees and staff members, stimulating a sense of mission among colleagues, reinforcing their professional effort, promoting cohesiveness and cooperation, and maintaining high staff morale
- *Participatory Leadership Skills.* Involving staff members in policy decisions, consulting with them, valuing their input, and keeping them informed
- *Advocacy Skills.* Protecting the professional roles of all staff members, standing up with impartiality for the rights of individuals and groups
- *Management Skills.* Making effective use of existing institutional structures to facilitate work performance of staff

---

*Adapted from: G.L. Lippitt and R. Lippitt, *The Consulting Process in Action*. San Diego, CA, University Associates, 1978. Used with permission.

members: short-term and long-term planning, acquisition of needed resources and technical equipment, ongoing maintenance of facilities, etc.

Sensitivity to Nonverbal Communication

Attention should always be given to nonverbal communication that significantly modifies the meaning of verbal communication. Readers who wish to review the various forms of body language and nonverbal communication are referred to Mehrabian's (1972) book, *Nonverbal Communication* or to a summary provided by Ivey and Simek-Downing (1980) in their volume, *Counseling and Psychotherapy*.

ADEQUATE WORK EXPERIENCE

This third component in the profile of a helping professional is important since it heightens the level of professional maturity and familiarity with the "real world" of counselor functioning. Work experience is important for consultants and even more for counselor supervisors, if they wish to stimulate confidence in their ability to deal with complex issues. It makes little sense for counselors to be supervised by someone who has only theoretical knowledge of the problems that they face or who has not been adequately exposed to job-related tensions that they experience.

The length and intensity of experience required for consultants and supervisors depend on the severity of the problems they are likely to encounter and on the degree of responsibility (full or shared) they have to assume. In the case of administrative counselor supervisors, two useful rules should be followed:

1. Supervisors should have personally carried out most of the professional activities they are to supervise, and they should have done so over a sufficient period of time to understand the process of such activities and their impact upon all who may be involved.

2. Supervisors should have proven their ability to handle work loads comparable to those expected of the practitioners whom they are to supervise.

Personal experiences help consultants and supervisors form a more realistic perspective on the pressures most practitioners (counselors, teachers, social workers, and other case workers) have to bear. For that reason, many supervisors wish to carry at least a limited case load or occasionally substitute for counselors who are absent for a period of time.

In the field of consultation, successful professionals have often stated that every new case has been a helpful learning experience for them. This position is underscored by Brown, Wyne, Blackburn, and Powell (1979) who perceive personal experimentation as the primary learning process of most persons currently involved in consulting work.

SUMMARY

1. The personalities of successful professional helpers match a basic profile that contains personal traits and values, professional attitudes and skills, and adequate work experiences.

2. The personal traits of helpers include self-awareness, self-acceptance, maturity, adequate intellectual ability, decisiveness, and concreteness.

3. Their values are humanistic with strong underlying altruistic sentiments. Their primary commitment is to the individual person. However, they balance the needs of individuals with those of society.

4. Their professional attitudes are generated by a combination of competence and ethical integrity.

5. Among the ethical tenets mandated by the American Personnel and Guidance Association are commitment, responsibility, truthfulness in stating one's competencies, primary concern for the welfare of the client, appropriate expression of values, and confidentiality.

6. Counseling skills are listed in inventory form, since teaching them is not the purpose of this book. It is assumed that readers are familiar with such skills. Their use in consultation and supervision will be explained in subsequent chapters.

7. Adequate work experiences are of vital importance in the helper's profile. They are needed since they stimulate professional maturity and give assurance to others of the helper's competence and understanding of real life situations.

REFERENCES

Adler, A.: Individual psychology. In Murchison, C. (Ed.): *Psychologies of 1930.* Worcester, MA, Clark University Press, 1930, pp. 395-405.

Allport, G.W.: *Pattern of Growth in Personality.* New York, Holt, Rinehart and Winston, 1961.

*APGA: Ethical standards. *Guidepost* (supplement), 1981.

*Brammer, L.M.: *The Helping Relationship: Process and Skills,* 2nd ed. Englewood Cliffs, NJ, Prentice-Hall, 1979.

Brown, D., Wyne, M.D., Blackburn, J.E., and Powell, W.C.: *Consultation: Strategy for Improving Education.* Boston, Allyn and Bacon, 1979.

*Combs, A.W., Avila, D.L., and Purkey, W.W.: *Helping Relationships.* Boston, Allyn and Bacon, 1971.

Combs, A.W., and Snygg, D.: *Individual Behavior.* New York, Harper and Row, 1959.

Dinkmeyer, D., and Carlson, J.: *Consulting: Facilitating Human Potential and Change Processes.* Columbus, OH, Merrill, 1973.

Erikson, E.H.: *Identity: Youth and Crisis.* New York, Norton, 1968.

*Frankl, V.E.: *Man's Search for Meaning.* New York, Simon and Schuster, 1970.

*Ivey, A.E., and Simek-Downing, L.: *Counseling and Psychotherapy: Skills, Theories, and Practice.* Englewood Cliffs, NJ, Prentice-Hall, 1980.

Lippitt, G., and Lippitt, R.: *The Consulting Process in Action.* LaJolla, CA, University Associates, 1978.

Mehrabian, A.: *Nonverbal Communication.* Chicago, Aldine, 1972.

*Quinn, I.T.: *Consultation Skills for Pupil Personnel Services Staff.* Ann Arbor, MI, ERIC-CAPS, Clearinghouse, 1980.

Rogers, C.R.: *Client-Centered Therapy: Its Current Practice, Implications, and Theory.* Boston, Houghton Mifflin, 1951.

*Shostrom, E.L.: *Man, the Manipulator.* Nashville, Abingdon Press, 1967.

---

*Recommended readings

CHAPTER 4

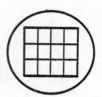

PROCESS AND STAGES
IN CONSULTATION AND SUPERVISION

I N the first two chapters we have compared the definitions of counseling, consultation, and supervision and have explored their mutual relationships. Although they differ from each other, all three activities fall in the area of human services. In counseling, there is a dyadic relationship between counselor and client. In consultation, a triadic relationship exists between consultant, consultee, and a third party who is the ultimate consumer of the service (*see* Figure 4-1). In supervision, the relationship can be either triadic or dyadic, depending on the supervisor's decision to act as consultant or counselor.

In this chapter, we will explore the processes of consultation and supervision and their typical stages of development. As we have noted earlier, supervisors use consultation as their chief strategy. Thus, the dynamics of the two helping activities are highly interrelated. Their processes and their developmental stages are marked by close parallels.

THE PROCESS DIMENSION
IN CONSULTATION AND SUPERVISION

A process can be defined as a series of continuous actions that proceed through stages and bring about certain outcomes. In this sense, every human activity and life itself is a process. Yet,

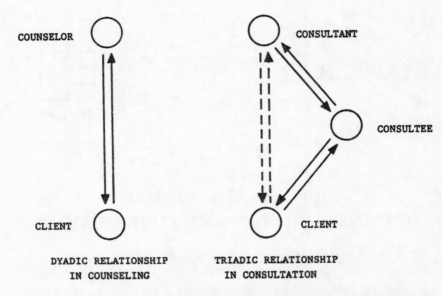

Figure 4-1. Counseling and Consultation. Solid lines indicate direct assistance, and dotted lines indicate indirect assistance.

when we speak of the process of a helping intervention, we refer not only to the course of gradual development through stages but to a special quality of the interaction. Goodstein (1978) draws two basic distinctions: one between process and product; the other between process and content.

In *product-oriented interventions*, the outcome is a tangible product. For instance, in industry, consultants are hired to come up with specific plans for the installation of a new telecommunication system or for the adoption of a more efficient bookkeeping method. At the conclusion of the consultation process, the outcome is finalized, at least for the time being.

In *process-oriented interventions*, the outcome is not a neatly packaged product but rather an extension of the helping process itself. For instance, a consultant working with teachers of a school will initiate certain new procedures to increase faculty communication and to stimulate fresh attitudes among faculty members. After the consulting work has been completed, the initiated processes continue. This principle applies to the entire field of human services in which the product of the intervention is a process.

In *content-oriented interventions*, emphasis is placed exclusively on facts and data, on the content of communication. While this emphasis is appropriate in itself, it often leads to a slanted view of the total scene. The concrete situation involves not only hard data but also feelings of people, individual and group values, the *flow* of communication, and other variables. The process orientation allows the helping professional to perceive the entire range of dynamics in depth rather than merely the surface of a given situation. For instance, a supervisor who depends exclusively on written reports from the agency's staff, who schedules only infrequent staff meetings, and who seldom meets individually with staff members will form a slanted view of the agency's functioning. While the statistical reports look encouraging, there may be a great deal of dissatisfaction among staff members.

Only process-oriented interaction between supervisor and staff can provide a comprehensive assessment that will uncover what really is occurring in the supervised department or agency. Important messages are revealed by the tone of voice, the eagerness or hesitancy of responses to certain questions, by body language, and other clues.

Schein (1978), who has pioneered the process approach in consultation, adds another important dimension to what has just been said. In his view, process consultation means that the client has to be involved in the diagnosis of the problem, in the setting of goals, in the exploration of alternatives, and in the eventual solution. The consultant does not assume ownership of the client's problem. Instead, the problem that belongs to the client is being resolved by a joint effort of consultant and client. Furthermore, sharing responsibility for the outcome is a therapeutic endeavor in itself, since it promotes client growth.

This approach is equally applicable to supervision. Most supervisors use their influence for stimulating self-directiveness of counselors under their jurisdiction, while sharing in the problem-solving process and offering encouragement. Such an approach promotes professional maturity and minimizes dependency.

Two other intervention models are in contrast with the process-oriented model. One is the *provision model* (Kurpius, 1978), which is frequently used in business consultation when the client system does not have the time or the qualified personnel to identify problems and find solutions. Schein (1978) calls this model "purchase of expertise." The client system seems to imply, "Here is the problem, bring me back an answer, and tell me how much it will cost" (p. 340).

The so-called *doctor-patient model* is based on the assumption that the client is sick and unable to cope and that the responsibility for the diagnosis and treatment must be assumed by a professional helper. While this approach includes provisions for making the client more self-reliant, it is questionable that this will happen. Rather, it is likely that the client will maintain dependency on the master helper for some time.

Conclusions on the Process Dimension

1. Consultation and supervision are helping processes. As is true of any process, they develop gradually and in sequential stages.

2. However, the process dimension has additional meaning that relates to the quality and to the outcomes of the helping interaction.

3. A process-oriented interaction, by its nature, stimulates active participation of the client or client system. It emphasizes exploration of intangible factors, such as people's feelings, attitudes, and values, which may be below the surface but significantly influence any given situation.

4. However, process-oriented interaction does not preclude directive approaches to be taken by professional helpers when needed. It does not ignore hard data and objective information, though it does not depend on such input exclusively.

5. The process dimension implies that the outcome of the interaction is not tangible and final as, for example, in surgery. The outcome is an ongoing process initiated within the client or client system through the helping intervention.

6. The outcome of the helping intervention has to be planned with care to assure both concreteness and flexibility. Lack of concreteness leads to aimless and unproductive busywork. On the other hand, lack of flexibility artificially restricts the scope of the outcome and hinders the development of potential benefits that may be available to the client or client system.

STAGES IN HELPING INTERVENTIONS

All helping interventions proceed gradually through a series of stages. These are developmental steps that lead from the first encounter between helper and helpee to the conclusion of the relationship. The distance between these two points is covered by a forward movement that involves establishment of rapport, identification of problems, and exploration of alternatives and eventually leads to a decision.

The stages are epigenetic in nature, each building upon the cumulative accomplishments of all previous stages. If the tasks inherent to one of the previous stages have not been sufficiently carried out, the defect will invariably appear. The consulting process may have to be temporarily drawn back to that stage before proceeding further. We shall see that there is a close similarity between the stages involved in counseling and those found in consultation and supervision.

Stages in Consultation

Many authors, when discussing stages of the consultation process, focus primarily on institutional consultation; others propose parallel stages for consultation with individual clients and with institutions. There are valid reasons for linking individual and institutional consultation. With the exception of independent professionals in private practice, all consultees are operating within some institutional structure. Thus, helping them as individuals cannot be effectively accomplished without a degree of involvement with the institution.

The framework of developmental stages that follows can be used for consultation with individuals, groups, and institutions.

First Stage: Decision to Assume the Consulting Task

Unless consultants actively search for new work opportunities, the initiative for consultation usually comes from potential clients who seek assistance or from a third party, perhaps a satisfied consumer of consulting services who recommends the contact. This stage offers the initial test of the consultants' good judgment. Before entering the relationship, consultants have to assess their readiness and ability to work with the specific problem areas and to assist the clients or client systems.

Such assessment has to cover not only one's skills and the availability of time but also personal values and biases regarding the individuals and organizations involved (Kurpius, 1978). Consultants should ask themselves whether they can maintain the necessary objectivity and impartiality; this is particularly important if they are to work as inside consultants on a problem within their own organization. Before accepting any consulting task, consultants should disclose to clients the extent of their qualifications and form a general idea about the clients' circumstances, needs, and readiness for change (Lippitt and Lippitt, 1978).

Second Stage: Entry, Rapport Building, Contract

After the decision has been made to establish a consulting relationship, consultants have to initiate the process of building rapport with the individual client or with key people in the organization, especially those who are natural leaders — articulate and respected by others. Typical helper attitudes and verbal and nonverbal communication skills (discussed in Chapter 3) are to be employed, as is done in the initial stages of counseling.

Caplan (1964) feels that in institutional consultation, the support of management has to be assured from the very beginning. Ground rules of the consultation process are to be established, roles of participants are to be clarified, and a tentative timetable is to be agreed upon. Lippitt and Lippitt (1978) add a rather pragmatic consideration: "It is crucial to determine who the client system really is, particularly to discover whether there is a difference between the client system and the individual or office that pays the bill" (p. 16).

Caplan (1970) recommends that a contract be drawn up that would summarize the outcomes of all preliminary discussions. This does not have to be a legal document. A letter of agreement signed by consultant and consultee will suffice. Such a written agreement ususally spells out (1) the obligations of the consultant, i.e. work involved in the project, limits of confidentiality, etc., (2) the obligations of the client or client system (degree of staff cooperation, clerical assistance, consulting fee, etc.), and (3) the desired outcomes (in generic rather than in specific terms). It goes without saying that the written agreement, while important, should be kept brief and simple; also, that a formal agreement is needed only for contractual consulting work.

Third Stage: Exploration and Diagnosis of the Problem

Prior to making a diagnosis of the problem, a wide area of concerns and circumstances even remotely related to the suspected problem has to be explored. In the course of such an exploration, the perspective on the problem frequently changes. The previously suspected focal issue emerges as a symptom of another, perhaps more fundamental, problem that has to be faced (Kurpius, 1978).

Although various approaches can be used for the in-depth exploration of the problem area, top priority should be given to interviewing people who are directly linked with the problem area. A series of interviews of this nature will provide basic factual information and shed light on attitudes and feelings linked with the problem situation. Additionally, the consultant needs to spend sufficient time observing ongoing processes of the client system, reviewing role descriptions of involved personnel, and analyzing other available records.

A helpful practical guide for methodically exploring any problem area follows:

Who: Is the problem generated by people, and if so, by which individuals or groups within the client system?

What: What appears to be the problem? Is it manifested by individual or group behavior? Is it an ongoing conflict, perhaps a clash between individual and institutional goals?

How: Is the problem related to methodology or principles guiding the activities and processes within the client system?

Under Which Circumstances: Is the problem related to particular circumstances that may or may not be avoided?

When: Do time-related factors contribute to the problem, e.g. is the severity of the problem typically increased at certain times of the day, of the month, or of the year?

Where: Is the problem related to the physical environment or work setting?

Why: While reviewing the total picture, which of the previous factors, or their combination, is emerging as the *fundamental cause* of the problem and of its present intensity?

Having explored the problem area from various aspects, the consultant and client (or client system) are usually ready to answer the *why*, which is the diagnosis of the focal issue that constitutes the problem. If the *why* cannot be answered, the individual factors that may have contributed to the current situation need to be explored further. Lippitt and Lippitt (1978) recommend the force-field diagnostic model for identifying the relative strength of forces that facilitate a development and of forces that seem to impede it. This approach will be discussed more extensively in Chapter 10 of this volume (*see* Figure 10-1).

Fourth Stage: Setting of Goals

By diagnosing the problem, consultant and client have established where they currently are. By setting goals, they announce where they intend to be. To arrive at the solution of the problem, they need to know the direction in which they want to move. Walz and Benjamin (1978) speak of "a future-imaging warm-up" in which people project their fondest hopes and image their work to be accomplished under the most favorable circumstances.

It is at this stage that the consultant must help strike a healthy balance between ideal expectations and realistic considerations. Both unrestrained dreaming and pedestrian mentality have to be avoided. However, it is preferable to err by setting goals that are too modest than by setting unrealistic goals.

Fifth Stage: Exploration of Options

While the goals are clearly identified and agreed upon, there are numerous ways of pursuing them. It is important to explore all available options and to involve as many people as possible in this exploration. The options relate to the type of interventions that can be applied and to the modalities of solutions to be attempted. For instance, the interventions can be person-oriented, issue-oriented, or behavior-oriented, either in pure form or in combination. The solutions can involve changes in priorities, streamlining of procedures, personnel changes, structural modifications, and other measures.

The task at hand is to select the most effective intervention (or combination of interventions) that will lead to the best solution consistent with the goals agreed upon earlier. The exploration of options lays the groundwork for the decision-making process.

Sixth Stage: Making and Implementing a Decision

The process and outcome of this stage is the culmination of all preceding stages. The nature of the decision will depend to a significant degree on the quality of diagnostic and exploratory efforts and on the appropriateness of chosen goals. However, even a well-balanced decision involves some risks as it may generate unforeseen consequences.

To minimize these risks, the decision must contain an operational plan – who does what and how – and an assessment of needed resources. If the operational plan is clear and realistic, chances for its successful implementation are significantly enhanced. However, since most behaviors are ingrained and are cyclical in nature, the pattern is not easily broken, and there may be a latent resistance to implementing the new course of action (Blake and Mouton, 1976). Thus, the consultant has to press for prompt implementation of the decision and to remind all involved persons of their earlier commitments and of the benefits they can expect from the change.

Seventh Stage: Evaluation of Final Outcomes

After the decision has been implemented, the consultant should remain in touch with the client or client system, monitor the progress of initiated changes, and encourage ongoing feedback from all persons involved in the decision. If, over a period of time, the outcomes prove to be consistent with initial expectations, no additional intervention is needed. However, in some cases the outcomes are not fully satisfactory, perhaps because new, unforeseen circumstances outside of the client system have emerged. In such cases, the originally chosen course of action has to be modified.

If, occasionally, the implementation of the decision turns out to be impractical or even counterproductive, this setback can be overcome by recycling the consulting process. Some individuals or groups may have been left out during the early stages, the diagnosis may have been incorrect, the selected goals may have been unrealistic, or the exploration of options may have been incomplete. A systematic review of the consulting stages, a reevaluation of various earlier conclusions, and the use of an alternative problem-solving approach will invariably lead to a decision that *can* be implemented. In such cases, it is particularly important that the consultant maintains his or her decisiveness, tact, and persistence.

Eighth Stage: Termination of the Consulting Project

The withdrawal of the consultant's support should be gradual, and provisions should be spelled out for additional consultation opportunities if the need arises. Periodic review contacts should be scheduled a while to assure continuity of the initial prograss. If a formal termination or farewell party is held, the consultant should counteract the impression that the process of renewal, the real outcome of the consultation project, has been completed. Rather, the responsibility for the renewal process now rests with the client organization.

Applying This Sequence to Supervision

The developmental sequence of consultation can be applied to supervisory activities with certain modifications. To do so, we have to be aware of the differences that exist between consultation and supervision processes:

1. Every consultation project has a clear time frame in which it operates, with a target date set for its completion. In contrast, supervision is usually an ongoing process that is limited only by the tenure of the supervisor or the supervisee, except in the case of interns or practicum trainees.

2. As a rule, consultants offer their services to individual consultees or client systems in response to a request and for a fee. Consultant and consultee are in a *staff relationship*, which is based on the consultant's expertise rather than on real power over the consultee. In contrast, counseling practitioners or graduate students in counselor education usually have no choice regarding the persons who will supervise them. In addition, supervisors outrank the supervisees by virtue of their appointment or instructorship. The supervisor-supervisee relationship is based on the *line model*, i.e. the supervisor possesses real power in addition to the expertise required for the supervisory position.

3. Consultation is a helping process with its own inherent functions, and its stages are well defined. In contrast, counselor supervision incorporates several helping processes and their functions, in particular, counseling, consultation, teaching, and evaluation. There is an overlap of these processes and functions, which are applied concurrently or intermittently. Therefore, the stages in supervision are not identical with the stages in consultation. Figure 4–2 offers a graphic description of the overlapping processes and functions.

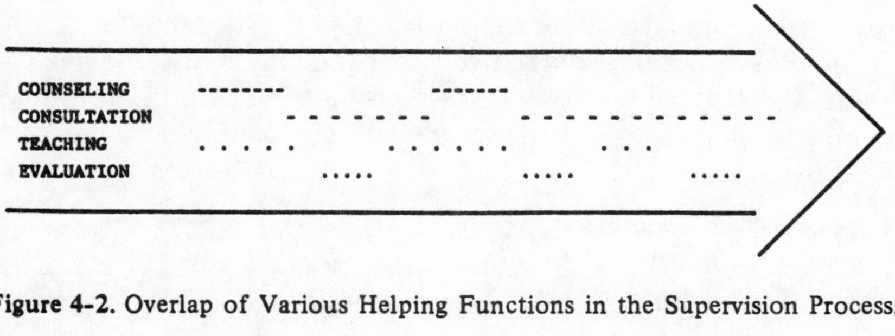

Figure 4-2. Overlap of Various Helping Functions in the Supervision Process.

Stages in Supervision

Each of the functions used in supervision has its own developmental dynamics. However, the following stages in the *total development* of the supervision process can be identified.

First Stage: Entry, Rapport Building

The dynamics of this stage approximate the rapport-building phase in consulting. Additionally, the supervisor and supervisee may share each other's preferences of counseling strategies and their mutual professional interests.

Second Stage: Beginning Consultation — Goal Setting, Teaching

Since problems are not always encountered in the early stages of supervision, the order of stages applied in consultation is reversed. Setting of goals is always of primary importance and usually precedes problem solving. The general goals of the counselor's professional growth and the specific therapeutic priorities of the institution (e.g. school, social agency, and mental health center) are clarified. The prevalent needs of the client population are discussed.

The consultation model of supervision focuses both on helping to solve problems of clients and on upgrading the professional functioning of the supervised counselor. It is similar to personalized and interactional teaching as it facilitates professional growth of the supervisee through trustful dialogue with the supervisor.

Third Stage: Ongoing Consultation — Problem Solving

When problems arise, the supervisor and counselor explore them and arrive at a mutually acceptable solution. During professional training and in the early phases of employment, the supervised counselor is relatively dependent on the supervisor's assistance. It is the supervisor's responsibility to help the counselor gradually develop a higher degree of self-confidence and self-directiveness.

Fourth Stage: Evaluation

To monitor the skill-building progress and the overall effectiveness of the counselor, the supervisor and the counselor jointly engage in evaluation processes at various stages of supervision.

Self-evaluation by the counselor is important for gaining insight, while feedback by the supervisor provides a major incentive for the counselor's professional growth. Each evaluation is to assess the degree to which the goals set earlier in the supervisory sequence have been attained.

Littrell, Lee-Borden, and Lorenz (1979) propose a useful supervision model designed for practicum and internship experiences. The stages of this model include: (1) relationship building, goal setting, and contract (goals, methods, and evaluation procedures); (2) counseling and teaching, i.e. dealing with personal problems or professional deficiencies of the student; and (3) consultation approaches that stimulate (4) self-supervision. Another interesting model of counselor-trainee supervision, presented by Delaney (1978), is designed to reflect the counseling process.

SUMMARY

1. Consultation and supervision are perceived as developmental processes progressing through stages.

2. The process dimension has an additional meaning: It places consultation and supervsion in contrast with content- or product-oriented activities.

3. The outcome of a process-oriented interaction is the continuation of the initiated therapeutic process; its success depends on the active cooperation of helper and helpee.

4. Eight stages of consultation have been identified, with special emphasis on a practical problem-solving methodology.

5. The stages of supervision are a modification of the general developmental pattern of consultation.

REFERENCES

Blake, R.R., and Mouton, J.S.: *Consultation.* Reading, MA, Addison-Wesley, 1976.

Caplan, G.: *Principles of Preventive Psychiatry.* New York, Basic Books, 1964.

Caplan, G.: *The Theory and Practice of Mental Health Consultation.* New York, Basic Books, 1970.

*Delaney, D.J.: Supervising counselors-in-preparation. In Boyd, J.D. (Ed.): *Counselor Supervision: Approaches, Preparation, Practices.* Muncie, IN, Accelerated Development, 1978, pp. 343-374.

*Goodstein, L.D.: *Consulting with Human Service Systems.* Reading, MA, Addison-Welsey, 1978.

Kurpius, D.: Consultation theory and process: An integrated model. *Personnel and Guidance Journal, 56*:335-338, 1978.

*Lippitt, G., and Lippitt, R.: *The Consulting Process in Action.* LaJolla, CA, University Associates, 1978.

*Littrell, J.M., Lee-Borden, N., and Lorenz, J.: A developmental framework for counseling supervision. *Counselor Education and Supervision, 19*: 129-136, 1979.

*Schein, E.H.: The role of the consultant: Content expert or process facilitator? *Personnel and Guidance Journal, 56*:339-343, 1978.

Walz, G.R., and Benjamin, L.: A change agent strategy for counselors functioning as consultants. *Personnel and Guidance Journal, 56*:331-334, 1978.

---

*Recommended readings

CHAPTER 5

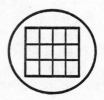

STRATEGIES IN CONSULTATION
AND SUPERVISION

BEFORE we discuss the strategies used in consultation and supervision, it may be useful to reexamine the diagram of the Three-Dimensional Intervention Model (*see* Figure 2-3). All three strategies, identified by Roman numerals, can be used both in consulting and supervisory interventions. They are suitable for dealing with any of the targets of intervention, identified by Arabic numerals, and for addressing any of the four types of issues, identified by capital letters.

COMBINED USE OF STRATEGIES

Helping strategies are frequently used in combination. During rapport building, while developing a consulting or supervisory relationship, the affective-supportive strategy is preferable. However, as the relationship enters the problem-solving, decision-making, and implementation stages, cognitive-objective and behavioral approaches are largely the strategies of choice.

Another reason for using a combination of strategies lies in the nature of the problem to be addressed. For instance, when the problem area involves both personal attitudes and organizational issues, a single strategy will not suffice. Dealing simultaneously with behavioral variables and with organizational issues calls for a skillful combination of strategies. Also, we have to re-

member that most consultants and supervisors develop their preferred personal style, usually a combination of strategies, which
reflects their personality, values, and experiences.

The entire spectrum of helping attitudes and skills (covered in
Chapter 3) is of importance, no matter which strategy, or combination of strategies, helpers use. Views that a humanistic orientation is incompatible with issue-oriented and behavioral strategies,
or that person-oriented interventions fail to promote concrete
outcomes, are not supported by empirical evidence. Successful
outcomes of most helping processes result from the helper's
harmonious blending of genuine concern for people, practical
sense, and enterprising behavior. In this chapter, the three proposed strategies are described in terms of counseling and personality theories that are familiar to most counselors.

PERSON-ORIENTED STRATEGY

This strategy focuses on people as individuals rather than on
client systems. It deals primarily with subjective factors, such as
feelings, personal values, and aspirations rather than with objective data. Its underlying assumptions are linked to phenomenology
and existentialism, both of which emphasize the uniqueness and
subjectivity of every person. What the individual accepts as reality
is contained within his or her phenomenal field, which is the only
reality that a person directly experiences (Combs and Snygg,
1959). The core of the phenomenal field is the phenomenal
self, whose center is the self-concept.

Role of the Self-Concept

The person-oriented strategy attaches great importance to a
person's self-concept. A negative self-concept stifles the person's
ability to cope, while a positive self-concept stimulates personal
growth and behavioral effectiveness. The self-concept of a person
is enhanced if he or she is accepted with empathy and unconditional positive regard (Meador and Rogers, 1979). Such acceptance results from the helper's willingness to assume the helpee's
perspective and view the situation from the helpee's vantage point
(Combs and Snygg, 1959). This does not imply that the helper

always agrees with the helpee's perspective or considers it accurate and useful. The helper merely recognizes it as being real to the helpee. For instance, a consultant may have documented evidence that the teacher's perception of the principal's decision is highly biased; nevertheless, he or she listens to the complaints without disputing them.

Unconditional Positive Regard

The helper communicates positive regard by focusing on the personal worth of the client, without placing any conditions. This does not always imply approval of the client's behavior, which may be recognized as the real source of the problem.

This person-oriented strategy, although similar to the approach of Rogerian therapy, is not identical with it. The helper listens, reflects, and clarifies the client's verbal and nonverbal communication. He or she also interprets the content and feelings of the client's messages and is willing to lead the client when appropriate. While the main emphasis is placed on the affective domain, the client's cognitive processes are not ignored. Every person's life-style, value structure, and coping behavior reflect his or her unique blend of thinking and feeling. The focus of this strategy is the *total person* of the client as perceived by himself or herself. Figure 5-1 presents the perimeter of the person-oriented strategy.

Encouragement

Another emphasis of the person-oriented strategy is on helping the client through encouragement. Caplan (1970) observes that lack of self-confidence is one of the major problems among professional workers, e.g. new teachers in a school system or junior nurses in public health agencies. In his view, the consultant should provide ego support and smooth the client's path to other supportive figures. This is a useful approach, as long as it does not lock the client into a long-term dependency on others.

Encouragement provides ego support without generating dependency on others. It helps clients look for the source of support within themselves rather than in others and gradually become self-supportive (Dinkmeyer and Carlson, 1973; Dreikurs and Grey, 1970). Encouragement focuses on people as they are,

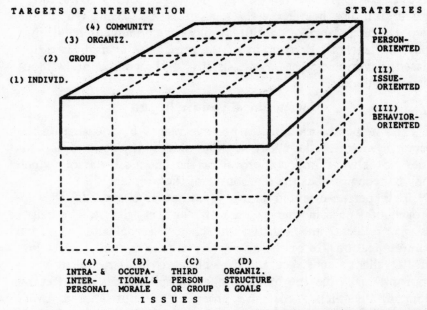

Figure 5-1. The Perimeter of the Person-Oriented Strategy (Solid Lines) within the Three-Dimensional Intervention Model (Dotted Lines). Although all targets of intervention can be addressed, the strategy focuses on individuals, either by themselves or as members of groups, organizations, or the community.

shows faith in them, and stimulates a "can-do" attitude. Recognition is given primarily for the individual's effort, with less concern for the degree of success. A supervisor, having observed a counselor work with a group, might say, "I agree with you that the group isn't very cohesive as yet. But I noticed how hard you tried to make the withdrawn members participate. What else do you think may be helpful?"

Encouragement should not be confused with praise, which places emphasis on the product or on excelling over others, rather than on the person's effort. Soltz (1967) points out that praise has an undesirable effect on personality development. Children who are frequently praised retain the need for praise through their adult lives. Their effectiveness, their ability to cope, and their self-image are in constant jeopardy.

Encouragement is particularly helpful when we are consulting or supervising people whose self-esteem is overly dependent on the approval of others or on measurable success in their work. Through encouragement, we help them develop additional ego strength and self-directiveness.

Confrontation

There are some who need to become aware of unresolved ambiguities or contradictions in their lives. Such contradictions may exist between their statements and their feelings or between their professed principles and their behavior. Consultants and supervisors can help resolve such contradictions through nonthreatening confrontations that stimulate insight, self-awareness, and personality integration.

A person's unresolved contradictions often result in ineffective job-related behavior. For instance the manager of a large employment agency may strongly believe in the value of participatory leadership, but he frequently fails to consult with midlevel supervisory personnel before initiating procedural changes affecting their departments. This generates complaints and adversely affects morale. At first sight, the problem seems to be organizational. In reality, it is an intrapersonal problem of the manager. It is up to the consultant to confront the manager with the contradiction between his professed management policy and his failure to implement it. The timing and style of confrontation are crucial factors that have to be considered.

The person-oriented strategy, although primarily used for dealing with personal issues, has a much wider range of applications. All issues addressed in consultation and supervision, e.g. third party issues, staff cohesion, work morale, and organizational structure, are directly or indirectly linked with the self-concept of a person.

ISSUE-ORIENTED STRATEGY

This strategy shares common elements with the reality therapy and trait and factor theory. It addresses the cognitive domain of clients and focuses on documented facts and issues that affect individuals and groups of people. Its approach is objective, primarily based on hard data, with less attention given to subjective opinions and feelings that people may express. Subjective input is accepted to the extent that it supplies additional information for objective assessment and interpretation.

The strategy is particularly useful for problem solving, planning, and evaluation. By itself, it is less effective for developing human relationships. Rapport building is best promoted by introducing at least some elements of the person-oriented strategy. However, once rapport has been established, the issue-oriented strategy may be used in pure form. The perimeter of the issue-oriented strategy is shown in Figure 5-2.

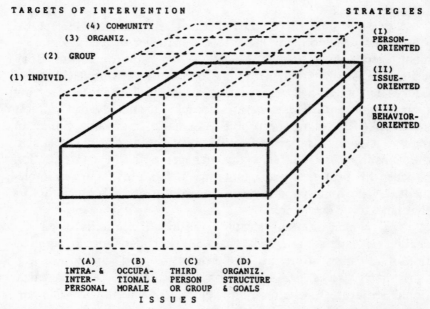

Figure 5-2. The Perimeter of the Issue-Oriented Strategy (Solid Lines) within the Three-Dimensional Intervention Model (Dotted Lines).

Rationale

The issue-oriented strategy relies on three premises: (1) Appropriate and proactive decisions are based on factual evidence supported by objective data. (2) The basic motivation of individuals and groups is self-interest, which involves the desire for self-preservation, self-enhancement, and security. (3) People are willing to assume new tasks or change their behavior only if they are persuaded by factual evidence that such action serves their self-interest.

Parenthetically, it should be added that all major psychological schools recognize self-interest as the primary human motivation. Maslow (1954, 1962) speaks of the need for self-actualization. Rogers (1951) calls it a "basic tendency and striving — to actualize, maintain, and enhance the experiencing organism" (p. 487).

Adler (1964) points out that self-interest is not identical with selfishness. In his view, the ultimate goal of "striving for superiority" is the achievement of social interest. Identification with others and healthy self-interest are compatible. One cannot exist without the other.

Operationally, the issue-oriented strategy places emphasis on (1) the collection of data and (2) the analysis and communication of data to clients. We will discuss these operational skills in some detail.

Collection of Data

Collecting data may begin even prior to the first contact with the client or client system. It often consists of the review of professional literature on the environment in which the helper will work and on typical problems to be found there. This advance preparation helps the professional acquire new information that may benefit the clients.

The process of collecting data in the field coincides with the diagnostic stage in consultation and supervision, which has been discussed in Chapter 4. Briefly restated, relevant data can be obtained through any of the following methods: (a) personal interviews, (b) direct observation of people on the job (e.g. teachers in the classrooms and agency personnel at staff meetings) and of available resources and their use, and (c) review of records, such as role descriptions of personnel, daily schedules of staff members, data on employee turnover, absenteeism, etc. Only for major consultation projects is it feasible to use questionnaires. These usually contain a combination of open-ended and closed questions and Likert-style scales that indicate the perceived intensity of certain variables.

Analysis and Communication of Data

As the collected data are analyzed, the more experienced professional will intuitively identify some obvious problem areas that need special attention. However, this initial clarity is often followed by a period of confusion as contradictory data surface. Caplan (1970) recommends to allow considerable time for this "state of greater or lesser confusion," and "to roam the field in response to whatever cues appear of intrinsic interest" (p. 241). A cognitive organization of all facets comes about eventually and leads to "gestalt closure" — *the total view of the issue*.

The professional shares the results of this cognitive organization with the clients in a clear and persuasive manner. He or she presents all pertinent data and offers clients an opportunity to question their accuracy and obtain clarification. This will help them accept the data as accurate and the evidence as valid. The professional must show genuine concern for the clients' welfare as he or she points out how they will benefit from a particular course of action. The decision to go ahead with the proposed plan has to be made jointly by the clients and the professional. The ultimate success of implementing the decision depends on the clients' conviction that the decision will serve their self-interest.

Applications

In the preceding discussion, the issue-oriented strategy has been interpreted primarily in terms of institutional consultation, but its application is much wider. It can be successfully used in counseling, in supervision, and in consultation with individuals. All issues that are listed on the horizontal axis of the Three-Dimensional Intervention Model (A, B, C, and D) can be addressed.

The issue-oriented strategy is particularly useful in counselor supervision. If a supervisor establishes a good track record of data-based administrative decisions and if he or she keeps his or her staff well informed, counselors working in the agency will maintain a high morale. In contrast, staff members who are asked to make personal sacrifices to help their agency survive a period of reduced funding will show no willingness to go along with the plan if they are not persuaded of the necessity for such sacrifices and of their interests being served in the long run.

BEHAVIOR-ORIENTED STRATEGY

This strategy focuses on observable behavior of individuals rather than on their feelings, self-awareness, or personal values. For instance, a behaviorally oriented supervisor would focus on the demonstrated skills and techniques rather than on intra-personal dynamics of the supervised counselor unless they are behaviorally expressed. The approach, based on Skinner's (1953) theory, is cognitive, empirical, and interventionist.

Helping interventions are seen as modifications of client behavior, and client growth is perceived in terms of learning new, more effective behavior patterns. Although consultees or supervisees may desire to attain agreed-upon goals, a degree of inertia and unrecognized resistance must be overcome prior to reaching these goals. This strategy helps overcome such obstacles, and therefore, is particularly useful for implementing decisions. The perimeter of the behavior-oriented strategy is shown in Figure 5-3.

I wish to add that although the behavior-oriented strategy is considered by some to be impersonal, mechanistic, or manipulative, it need not be so. Behaviorally oriented professionals know that their main goal is helping people, and many of them profess behavioral humanism. It is true that quantification of behavioral variables plays an important role in behavioral research. Thoresen and Coates (1980) emphasize that "research is treatment and treatment is research" (p. 10). However, the insistence on research need not detract from the helper's genuine caring.

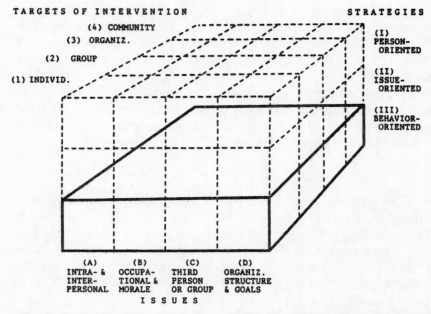

TARGETS OF INTERVENTION   STRATEGIES

(4) COMMUNITY

(3) ORGANIZ.

(2) GROUP

(1) INDIVID.

(I)
PERSON-
ORIENTED

(II)
ISSUE-
ORIENTED

(III)
BEHAVIOR-
ORIENTED

(A) INTRA- & INTER- PERSONAL	(B) OCCUPA- TIONAL & MORALE	(C) THIRD PERSON OR GROUP	(D) ORGANIZ. STRUCTURE & GOALS

I S S U E S

Figure 5-3. The Perimeter of the Behavior-Oriented Strategy (Solid Lines) within the Three-Dimensional Intervention Model (Dotted Lines).

Rationale

The behavior-oriented strategy promotes relatively rapid changes in behavior, and because of its empirical emphasis, lends itself to processes of evaluation. It is based on the following assumptions:

1. All human behavior occurs according to laws, some of which have been identified.
2. Human behavior is the product of objective determinants; it is learned and therefore can be unlearned.
3. Positive reinforcement is the most effective tool for changing ineffective into effective behavior.
4. Punishment is not considered useful for promoting desirable behavior changes.

Most behavioral counselors such as Bandura (1971), Wolpe (1958), and Krumboltz and Thoresen (1976) extend the principles of behavioral intervention to the affective domain, including such covert states as intrapersonal conflicts, anxiety, and depression. Since the behavioral approach deals only with observable behavior, the client's affective state is to be conceptualized in behavioral terms. Typically, the counselor asks, "What behavior does the client engage in while in a particular affective state?" rather than "What does the client feel?"

Helping Interventions

The behavior-oriented strategy in consultation and supervision makes use of applied behavioral analysis. This involves assessing the frequency, intensity, and duration of a behavior to establish the *behavioral baseline*. The next step is the analysis of influences exerted by third persons and by the environment that stimulate and/or maintain such behavior (Kanfer and Saslow, 1969). The professional then helps the client identify, in concrete terms, the desirable behavior that is to replace the present ineffective behavior. Then they jointly devise a learning program, typically involving reinforcement of desirable behavior and extinction of undesirable behavior (Osipow and Walsh, 1970). Finally, the outcomes of the learning program are evaluated. A behavioral helper systematically and consistently reinforces those behaviors of the helpee that approximate the agreed-upon behavioral objectives. This process is called *shaping*.

Emphasis on Social Modeling

Teaching new behavior through modeling has been successfully promoted by Bandura (1971). He and his associates have demonstrated that individuals who observe a specific behavior of another person are themselves likely to engage in a similar, if not identical, behavior. People even learn to combine behaviors observed in a number of models into new behavior patterns (Bandura, Ross, and Ross, 1961). Modeling has proven to be very useful for instructional purposes in counselor education and supervision (Brown, 1977; Perry, 1975).

When applying the principle of modeling to consultation and supervision, we conclude that the professional's behavior is of major importance in promoting self-enhancing (or regressive) behavioral changes in the helpees. This points out the degree of responsibility required of consultants and supervisors who serve as role models for their helpees.

THE PERSONALIZED APPROACH

While reviewing these three strategies, we may have recognized in each of them certain elements of our own — perhaps still developing — helping approach. As consultants and supervisors, we need to establish an operational framework that would parallel our counseling orientation and fit our personality, life-style, and value structure (Peterson and Krajewski, 1980; Halloway and Wolleat, 1981). It may be useful to initially choose one or two theoretical approaches to serve as the basis of such a framework. However, it would be counterproductive if loyalty to a theory would interfere with our spontaneous professional development or hinder us from using our own personality as a therapeutic instrument.

In the course of their careers, many counselors adopt elements from other theories, modify their earlier convictions, and adjust their professional orientation. They become increasingly eclectic, as is shown in the example of an individual helping style in Figure 5-4.

Obviously, there is no ideal eclectic approach that will suit everyone. However, a logical, consistent, and integrated brand of eclecticism can be employed as opposed to an uncritical and haphazard accumulation of unrelated bits and pieces of various theories. Our ability to choose the proper combination will depend on the degree of our self-awareness and the clarity of our value structure (Squires, 1978). The higher the level of congruence between our professional and personal self-concept, the greater our effectiveness as helping professionals.

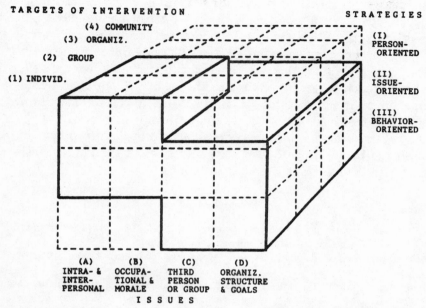

Figure 5-4. Example of an Eclectic Counseling and Consultation Approach. In dealing with intrapersonal and interpersonal issues, the helper uses person-oriented and issue-oriented strategies when counseling individuals and groups. In working as a consultant with individuals, groups, organizations, and the community, the helper uses the person-oriented strategy only for establishing rapport. Otherwise he or she relies heavily on issue- and behavior-oriented strategies. The helper's approach to supervision would be a combination of his or her counseling and consulting orientations.

SUMMARY

1. Helping strategies are used either in pure form or in combination. A blending of strategies is often inevitable because of the nature of the problem to be addressed.

2. The person-oriented strategy uses not only Rogerian but also other theoretical approaches. It focuses on the whole person of the client and emphasizes the subjective factors of individual behavior. It is particularly helpful for *rapport building*.

3. The issue-oriented strategy focuses on objective data that relate to existing issues rather than on subjective perceptions of

individuals. Emphasis is placed on presenting evidence that a particular course of action serves the self-interest of the client. The main strength of this strategy is its potential for *problem solving*.

4. The behavior-oriented strategy places emphasis on observable behavior rather than on covert facets of the individual's life. The approach is based on Skinner's theory of operant conditioning and on learning theories. It is most useful for *implementing agreed-upon decisions* of clients and professional helpers.

5. Consultants and supervisors should form their own personal approach based on various existing strategies; it should be consistent with their personal frame of reference.

REFERENCES

Adler, A.: *Superiority and Social Interest: A Collection of Later Writings.* Evanston, IL, Northwestern University Press, 1964.

*Bandura, A. (Ed.): *Psychological Modeling.* Chicago, Aldine-Atherton, 1971.

Bandura, A., Ross, D., and Ross, S.A.: Transmission of aggression through imitation of aggressive models. *Journal of Abnormal Social Psychology, 63:*575-582, 1961.

Brown, J.H.: Developing video models for counselor education. *Counselor Education and Supervision, 17:*131-136, 1977.

Caplan, G.: *The Theory and Practice of Mental Health Consultation.* New York, Basic Books, 1970.

Combs, A.W., and Snygg, D.: *Individual Behavior.* New York, Harper and Row, 1959.

*Dinkmeyer, D., and Carlson, J.: *Consulting: Facilitating Human Potential and Change Processes.* Columbus, OH, Charles E. Merrill, 1973.

Dreikurs, R., and Grey, L.: *A Parent's Guide to Child Discipline.* New York, Hawthorne, 1970.

Halloway, E.L., and Wolleat, P.L.: Style differences of beginning supervisors: An interactional analysis. *Journal of Counseling Psychology, 28:*373-376, 1981.

Kanfer, F.H., and Saslow, G.: Behavioral diagnosis. In Franks, C. (Ed.): *Assessment and Status of the Behavior Therapies and Associated Developments.* New York, McGraw-Hill, 1969, pp. 417-444.

*Krumboltz, J., and Thoresen, C. (Eds.): *Counseling Methods.* New York, Holt, Rinehart, and Winston, 1976.

*Maslow, A.: *Motivation and Personality.* New York, Harper and Row, 1954.

---

*Recommended readings

Maslow, A.: *Toward a Psychology of Being.* Princeton, NJ, Van Nostrand, 1962.

*Meador, B.D., and Rogers, C.R.: Person-centered therapy. In Corsini, R.J., et al.: *Current Psychotherapies.* Itasca, IL, Peacock, 1979, pp. 131-184.

*Osipow, S.H., and Walsh, W.B.: *Strategies in Counseling for Behavior Change.* New York, Appleton-Century-Crofts, 1970.

Perry, M.A.: Modeling and instructions in training for counseling empathy. *Journal of Counseling Psychology, 22*:173-179, 1975.

Peterson, A.V., and Krajewski, R.J.: Effective supervision of the counseling process. *Texas Personnel and Guidance Journal, 8*:97-103, 1980.

Rogers, C.R.: *Client-Centered Therapy.* Boston, Houghton Mifflin, 1951.

Skinner, B.F.: *Science and Human Behavior.* New York, Macmillan, 1953.

Soltz, V.: *Study Group Leader's Manual.* Chicago, Alfred Adler Institute, 1967.

Squires, D.A.: A phenomenological study of supervisors' perceptions of a positive supervisory experience. Unpublished doctoral dissertation, Pittsburg University, 1978.

Thoresen, C.E., and Coates, T.J.: What does it mean to be a behavioral therapist? In Thoresen, C.E. (Ed.): *The Behavior Therapist.* Monterey, CA, Brooks-Cole, 1980, pp. 1-41.

Wolpe, J.: *Psychotherapy by Reciprocal Inhibition.* Stanford, Stanford University Press, 1958.

---

*Recommended readings

Section II
WORKING WITH INDIVIDUALS AND GROUPS IN CONSULTATION AND SUPERVISION

THE interpersonal dynamics and processes in consultation and supervision are similar. The major difference between the two helping activities lies in the nature of the interpersonal relationship of helper and helpee — staff relationship in consultation and line relationship in supervision.

The following four chapters integrate the earlier presented information that covered the helper's attitudes and skills, the processes and stages of helping interventions, and the use of therapeutic strategies. These theoretical insights are translated into practical, operational patterns. Chapter 6 deals with individual consultation. Chapters 7 and 8 treat supervision of counselors in training and of counseling practitioners. Chapter 9 explains group approaches to consultation and supervision.

CHAPTER 6

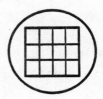

CONSULTATION WITH INDIVIDUALS

EARLIER in this volume it was pointed out that counselors can greatly expand the range of their helping interventions if they assume the role of consultants. A comparison of the perimeters of counseling and of consultation on the Three-Dimensional Intervention Model (*see* Figure 2-4 and Figure 2-6) demonstrates the degree to which the impact of counselors' work can be increased.

However, this broad societal impact hinges on the ability of counselors to work effectively with individual consultees. Institutions, and society itself, can be renewed only if key individuals and influential groups become convinced of the need for change. Miles and Hummel (1979) have found that most consulting work that counselors do is geared to individuals, in particular teachers, parents of clients, and administrators.

The aim of this chapter is to discuss the dynamics and processes involved in individual consultation. To meet the needs of the majority of readers, emphasis is placed on educational settings, but the insights gained are equally applicable to other human service systems. Figure 6-1 illustrates the perimeter of individual consultation. Issues dealt with include primarily occupational concerns and morale (B) and third person or group (C). The issue organizational structure (D), which may be part of the problem, will be treated extensively in Chapter 11. All three helping strategies — person-oriented (I), issue-oriented (II), and behavior-oriented (III) — are used in individual consultation.

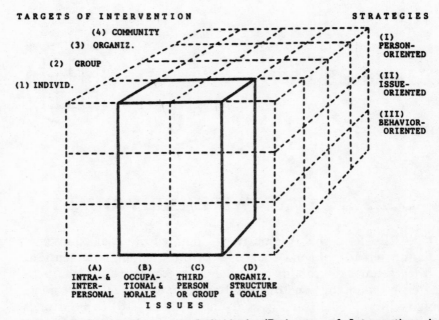

TARGETS OF INTERVENTION

(4) COMMUNITY
(3) ORGANIZ.
(2) GROUP
(1) INDIVID.

STRATEGIES

(I) PERSON-ORIENTED
(II) ISSUE-ORIENTED
(III) BEHAVIOR-ORIENTED

(A) INTRA- & INTER-PERSONAL
(B) OCCUPA-TIONAL & MORALE
(C) THIRD PERSON OR GROUP
(D) ORGANIZ. STRUCTURE & GOALS

ISSUES

Figure 6-1. Consultation with Individuals (Perimeter of Interventions in Solid Lines) within the Three-Dimensional Intervention Model (Dotted Lines).

TYPES OF TEACHER CONSULTATION

School counselors typically serve as internal consultants for teachers in their own schools. This function is considered part of the counselor's job, but teachers are not always aware of it. Gumaer (1980) points out that counselors have to be assertive in selling their consulting role to the teaching staff. They should be visible and available to teachers, treat them as fellow professionals, and should never talk down to them. He cautions counselors to avoid doing "too much too soon." By attaining small consultation successes, counselors gradually gain a reputation as consultants in their schools.

Occasionally, agency counselors are asked to work with teachers as outside consultants. In such cases, a request in writing should be obtained from the principal of the school. Before accepting the job, outside consultants should ask themselves whether they have the skills and motivation necessary for an effective consulting intervention. There are advantages and disadvantages to being an outside consultant. The outsider is more objective and usually stimulates trust among consultees by being free of involvement in internal disagreements. On the other hand, the outsider is less knowledgeable than the internal consultant about hidden problems that may be of major importance.

Caplan (1970) differentiates *consultee-centered* and *client-centered* case consultations. In both instances, the consultant works with the consultee for the benefit of a third person or a group. However, in consultee-centered interventions, primary emphasis is placed on upgrading the professional functioning of the consultee, e.g. the teacher. The teacher's present and future students are of course the ultimate beneficiaries of such interventions. In terms of the three-dimensional intervention model, the primary focus is on issue B, occupational concerns, morale. Issue C, third person or group, which has triggered the intervention, becomes a secondary focus (*see* Figure 6-2).

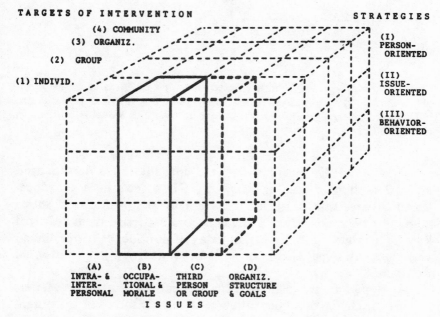

Figure 6-2. Perimeter of Consultee-Centered Consultation. Area of primary emphasis is marked in solid lines, and area of secondary emphasis is marked in bold dotted lines. The Three-Dimensional Intervention Model is outlined in thin dotted lines.

Conversely, client-centered case consultations emphasize the immediate needs of a particular client, student, or group (issue C). The focus on upgrading the consultee's level of professional functioning (issue B) is incidental and secondary (*see* Figure 6-3).

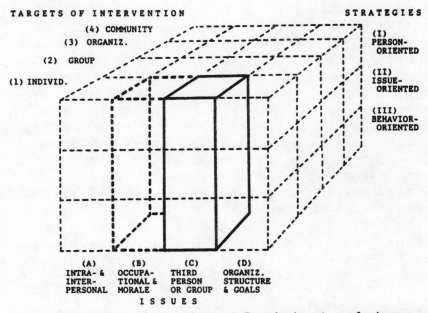

Figure 6-3. Perimeter of Client-Centered Consultation. Area of primary emphasis is marked in solid lines, and area of secondary emphasis is marked in bold dotted lines. The Three-Dimensional Intervention Model is outlined in thin dotted lines.

Briefly stated, consultee-centered consultation is personalized and interactional teaching. Caplan (1970) views it as an educational process that can effectively remedy the professional shortcomings of the consultee. Such shortcomings result from deficient knowledge, lack of skills, inadequate self-confidence (often linked with lack of experience), or lack of objectivity in professional judgment.

Applying these principles to educational settings, Meyers (1975) concludes that "consultee-centered consultation is a potentially powerful and economical way to improve the general effectiveness of some teachers" (p. 120). Improvements resulting from such consultation (to be called *teacher-centered* in this chapter) have been observed, particularly in the reduction of negative verbal behavior of teachers toward students (Meyers, Freidman, and Gaugham, 1975).

TEACHER-CENTERED CONSULTATION

Teacher-centered consultation is usually stimulated by apparent discipline problems in a classroom (Brown, Wyne, Blackburn, and Powell, 1979). The teacher may complain, the principal may have had complaints from others, or the counselor may have noticed the problem situation. What follows is an illustration of the interpersonal dynamics involving the consultant (counselor), the consultee (teacher), and the client system (children in the classroom) as they advance through the framework of eight developmental stages of the consultation process (*see* Chapter 4). The stages applicable to various types of consultation — individual, group, and organizational — must always be adjusted to the circumstances of a specific consulting intervention. Also, when using the suggested method for problem exploration, only those questions are to be selected that have a direct bearing on the current problem.

First Stage: Decision to Assume the Consulting Task

While conducting classroom guidance, the counselor has noticed an unusually high level of misbehavior in one of the second grade rooms. After class she asks the teacher, who is new in school whether there is anything she could do to help her. At first the teacher is defensive but later seeks the counselor's assistance. (In some cases, the counselor has to spend considerable energy to overcome a teacher's resistance.)

Second Stage: Entry, Rapport Building

Throughout the first meeting, the counselor encourages the teacher to express her feelings about the classroom situation. The teacher shows symptoms of discouragement, even distress. At times, she feels like a failure. Using the person-oriented strategy, the counselor reflects the teacher's feelings, keeps close eye contact, and communicates concern for the teacher by her body posture. A mutual decision is reached that the counselor observe the classroom activities and subsequently discuss her observations with the teacher.

Third Stage: Exploration and Diagnosis of the Problem

Direct Observation

The counselor senses a high level of restlessness and tenseness in the classroom atmosphere, a reflection of the teacher's own tenseness. Several of the children are acting out to attract attention of the class and to manipulate the teacher. By lecturing the misbehaving children, the teacher unwittingly reinforces this disruptive behavior. She has little time and energy left to focus on the entire class. The teacher's frustration clearly shows and, at times, borders on hostility. Many children look quizzically at the counselor, wondering what she thinks about their class.

Discussions of the Findings

The counselor later asks the teacher how she felt about having a stranger in class, and the teacher expresses embarassment about the children's acting-out. She names three boys and two girls as the "ringleaders." The counselor makes a mental note that the desks of these children were in the same area of the classroom.

Since the teacher needs encouragement, the counselor commends her efforts at keeping the class together in spite of the difficult circumstances. For additional exploration of the classroom situation, the counselor moves gradually to the issue-oriented strategy and uses the problem-solving pattern outlined in Chapter 4.

Who: The teacher has already mentioned the names of the children with behavior problems. Are there others who also cause problems? The counselor knows, of course, that the teacher's behavior is a major factor of the problem situation, but at this point, she does not focus on it.

What: During the classroom observation, the counselor saw children leave their seats without permission, talk without being recognized, and tease each other. She interprets such behavior to the teacher as ways by which children seek attention and try to assume power in class. Does this interpretation make sense to the teacher?

How: The counselor senses that rapport between her and the teacher has been established. She shifts attention to the teacher's behavior as the focal point of the problem. She inquires about the teacher's approach to classroom management. For instance, did she give the children rules for classroom behavior or tell them about consequences of their misbehavior? Is she consistent in dealing with the children? The teacher admits that this has been a weak area in her work. The counselor remains nonjudgmental.

Why: At this point the counselor involves the teacher in summarizing the various clues that have emerged and that provide a fairly comprehensive diagnosis of the problem:

1. The teacher lacks firmness and consistence.
2. She is held hostage to inappropriate classroom behavior resulting from the mistaken goals, which she unwittingly reinforces, of some children.
3. The principal troublemakers are sitting too close together in one corner of the room and tend to reinforce each other.
4. Most children do not seem to know what the rules of behavior are in their classroom and what consequences they can expect when misbehaving.
5. The teacher is not giving sufficient recognition and reinforcement to children who behave appropriately. She uses little encouragement and is predominantly negative in her comments.

Fourth Stage: Setting of Goals

The teacher speaks of the way she would like to have her class behave. The counselor listens and concurs with the teacher on the need for higher levels of responsibility, self-directiveness, and cooperation among the children. She also points out that the teacher needs to become firm and consistent in dealing with her class if she wants to attain these goals.

Fifth Stage: Exploration of Options

The counselor and teacher explore together various ways of promoting behavioral change in the classroom, such as assertive discipline proposed by Canter and Canter (1976), behavior modification, Adlerian methods, and reality therapy approaches. The counselor reminds the teacher of the need for changing the seating arrangement in class. Would the teacher like to participate in a teacher study group that will be formed in the later part of the semester? Would she be interested in doing some reading to gain a better understanding of classroom management? The counselor points out how the teacher would benefit from such efforts.

Sixth Stage: Making and Implementing a Decision

The teacher decides, and the counselor agrees, that a combination of the behavioral and Adlerian models will work out best for the class. The counselor, using the behavior-oriented strategy, reinforces the teacher's decision. It is important that the teacher experience at least limited success as soon as possible as a result of the steps to be taken:

1. The seating arrangement in the classroom is to be changed immediately.
2. With the counselor's help, a token system is to be introduced.
3. The teacher will consistently reinforce positive behavior and keep a check on her effort by taping a daily sample of her interaction with students. Self-observation has been shown by Piersell and Kratochwill (1979) to enhance the likelihood of behavioral change.
4. The teacher will present to the class a set of rules for classroom behavior.
5. After reading parts of Dreikurs and Cassel's (1974) book, *Discipline without Tears,* the teacher will use the Adlerian method of dealing with children's mistaken goals.
6. The counselor will observe the classroom interaction on a regular basis for several weeks and give the teacher feedback.

Seventh Stage: Evaluation of Final Outcomes

In the following month, the couselor observes the classroom every week. The new seating arrangement has proven helpful. The token economy has an ongoing, positive impact on the children's behavior. Acting-out has decreased in frequency, the classroom atmosphere is calmer, and the teacher is less tense. The counselor shares her observations with the teacher, who feels generally encouraged.

Both the counselor and teacher agree that the basic decision has been sound. However, they feel that the backup reinforcers in the token economy (the rewards that the tokens can purchase) need to be reassessed to make them more effective and consistent with the ultimate aim of self-control. The teacher says she feels comfortable with the new teaching style, but needs to be reminded not to slip back to her previous negative approach. For that purpose, the counselor recommends attendance at the meetings of a teacher study group.

Eighth Stage: Termination of the Consulting Project

The counselor gradually decreases the frequency of her classroom observations and eventually comes only for classroom guidance activities. She stays in touch with the teacher and discusses the classroom situation with her when necessary. Both she and the teacher recognize that the project is completed.

Conclusions and Inferences

1. Although the original incentive for the consulting intervention was the observed misbehavior of students, the focus soon shifted to the teacher's lack of skills. As a result of the teacher's improved professional functioning, the students themselves benefitted.

2. This was a process-oriented consultation concerned with interpersonal relations of teacher and students rather than with the curricular content. Its outcome was not a finalized product, but an ongoing human growth process involving the teacher and children. Having been stimulated in the course of the consultation process, the teacher has learned to do for her class what the counselor did jointly with her.

3. The consultation process moved from the subjective domain of the teacher, i.e. her perception of the classroom problem, to the objective domain, i.e. observation by the consultant, analysis of data, and to making and implementing a decision.

4. All three helping strategies were involved in the consultation process. The consultant first used the person-oriented strategy and later the issue- and behavior-oriented strategies.

5. The intervention has proven successful for the following reasons: (a) Rapport between the counselor and teacher has been established early and maintained throughout the intervention; (b) the teacher has been given an opportunity to get actively involved in all stages of the consultation process; (c) she perceived the required change in her behavior as being to her advantage; and (d) the decision contained a well-designed operational plan that was suitable for subsequent modification.

6. Occasionally, consultee-centered consultation helps uncover areas of professional weakness among other teachers and leads to remediation by in-service training or school-wide consultation programs. Jason, Ferone, and Anderegg (1979) offer an example of a teacher-centered consultation project for several teachers of the same school.

7. Consultee-centered consultation programs have a wide range of application in schools. Carr (1976) has shown that consultation with school principals can significantly increase teacher-group interaction at staff meetings.

CLIENT- OR STUDENT-CENTERED CONSULTATION

As was mentioned earlier, this consulting intervention focuses fully on the problem of the client or student. Lack of professional knowledge or skills in the consultee is not implied, although the consultee's professional functioning may eventually be enhanced as an indirect result of the consultation. In most cases, the consultee merely wants to talk over a difficult case and get a second opinion regarding the diagnosis and intended solution of a problem situation. In cases involving developmental problems of youth, a counselor is the logical resource person to be contacted.

The problems dealt with in client-centered consultation can involve all age groups. Some examples are underachievement, aggressive and antisocial behavior, low self-concept, mental handicaps, emotional handicaps, learning disabilities, multiple physical disabilities, giftedness, and trauma by loss of a parent or another significant person. Young children may additionally suffer from parental neglect or abuse or conversely from overattachment to parents and school phobia. Teenagers may have problems related to their identity, sex, alcohol and drug use, or motivation to remain in school.

Consultation Process

Client-centered consultation usually requires less time than a consultee-centered intervention. The earlier discussed eight stages are present in the process, although not always explicitly. Typically, the consultation is initiated by a teacher, administrator, or another professional in the school who presents the counselor with some problem involving one or more students. This is frequently done in general, even ambiguous terms; the counselor may not always be sure whether it is a request for consultation or an outright referral (Caplan, 1970).

Initial Stages

It is important for the counselor to find out the exact intention of the consultee, especially the degree to which the consultee wants the counselor to become directly involved. If the counselor is to assume a major part of responsibility for the case, he or she must have an opportunity to contact the client. By talking with the client, the counselor arrives at a clearer understanding of the problem. The comprehensive analysis of the problem is based on the consultee's input, on the client's verbal and nonverbal communication, and on information obtained from other sources regarding the client's home environment, current interests, social contacts, past history, etc.

Diagnosis, Exploration of Options

Occasionally, the counselor may have to seek additional knowledge of a complex problem area, e.g. substance abuse (Guydish, 1982), before offering a professional analysis of the main factors that have a bearing on the problem. If the counselor becomes convinced that the problem (e.g. severe schizophrenic reactions of a teenager) exceeds his or her level of expertise, he or she should recommend, without delay, referral of the client to another professional for diagnosis and treatment.

If the counselor decides to stay on the case, he or she and the consultee should jointly assess all data gathered for diagnosis. In some instances, a third person may be invited to the meeting to supply additional information or to clarify available data. When a final diagnosis of the problem is reached, the counselor and the consultee review available options prior to making a decision. In a school setting, the options usually include the following:

1. Counseling alone
2. Counseling combined with teacher and/or parent involvement or with another general education program
3. Referral to special services in the school system for additional diagnostic work and treatment. Before making any referral, the counselor and consultee should schedule a conference with the client's parents, since their permission is mandatory.

Making and Implementing a Decision, Referrals

The decision naturally emerges from the discussion of available therapeutic options. Once made, it should be implemented without delay. For instance, if counseling is indicated, individual sessions should be scheduled immediately, and the advisibility of group counseling should be explored. If teachers and parents are to be involved, the counselor may have to act as coordinator of their efforts and perhaps help develop a behavior modification contract for the student.

In cases in which the decision involves a referral, the counselor has to write (or participate in writing) a recommendation for referral. The recommendation should contain all relevant information that would help a third person understand the nature of the problem: objective data on the client's school performance and behavior, family background, etc. Caution must be used to avoid labeling the client or disclosing confidential information. When referring a client, it is wise for the counselor to withhold his or her tentative diagnosis. If the professional to whom referral is made wishes to obtain the counselor's diagnostic opinion, it is up to him or her to request it. Helpful suggestions on referral procedures and on writing various counseling reports are offered by Hollis and Donn (1973).

During the client's treatment, the counselor should keep in touch with the consultee (teacher, administrator, etc.), support the client's active participation in the treatment program, and check on the client's progress.

Evaluation of Outcomes, Termination

The counselor's direct observation and the feedback by consultee, client, and other persons involved provide a basis for evaluating the outcomes. If the outcomes are not fully satisfactory, the decision regarding treatment may have to be revised. The counselor should involve all persons connected with the case in the revision process. As we are well aware, some problems will never be *fully* resolved. However, virtually all problem situations can be improved, most of them significantly, if appropriate means and a dose of persistence are applied. Whenever a reasonable improvement of the student's problem area has been attained, the consultation is terminated.

CONSULTATION WITH PARENTS

Counselors, particularly those working in elementary schools, have frequent conferences with parents. These conferences are consultations, since they focus on the problems of children. If occasionally a parent brings up his or her own problem not directly related to the child, the parent needs counseling, not consultation. Some counselors provide a brief counseling interview for such parents to help them sort things out and to offer them suggestions about getting additional help. This is a useful approach, since the counselor provides short-term assistance and at the same time sets limits of professional services.

As with teachers, consultations with parents can be either client-centered or consultee-centered, depending on the principal focus of the intervention. If the primary focus is on a short-term (acute) problem of the child triggered by a recent traumatic experience, such as death in the family, divorce, a serious accident, or a disabling illness, the consultation is usually client-centered. It concentrates on the most effective way of helping the child overcome the temporary problem rather than on improving the parenting skills of the father or mother.

When dealing with a child's long-term intrapersonal or behavioral problem or with a chronic disability, the consultant usually follows the path of a consultee-centered intervention. The immediate focus is on helping the parent develop a better understanding of the child's condition and acquire more effective parenting skills. Since the consultation involves remedial teaching, the counselor may eventually recommend that the parents join a study group or attend a workshop. No matter what the child's problem may be, a general parenting skills course usually relieves that problem situation. Parents become more understanding and more responsive to the child's needs, and they improve their communication skills.

The Consultation Process

Parent consultation usually follows the same sequence of stages as teacher consultation, and teachers are frequently involved at certain stages along with parents. Since parents have a high level of emotional involvement in the child's problem, they tend to be less objective than teachers. This emotional involvement occasionally leads to tensions that may have to be overcome. Roe and Siegelman (1964) offer a useful classification of basic parental attitudes toward children:

1. Emotional overinvolvement with the child, which leads to overprotective or overdemanding attitudes
2. Avoidance of the child, which results in neglect or emotional rejection
3. Acceptance of the child, which may be either casual or loving

One of these parent-child relationships may emerge as predominant during the rapport-building stage as the counselor focuses on the parent's affective domain by listening, reflecting, and encouraging. The parent's verbal and nonverbal communication may cast new light on the problem at this early stage. It is wise to explore the child's problem in the context of the total family situation. Sonstegard (1964) proposes a ten-point interviewing model with a strong Adlerian emphasis on sibling configuration according to sex and age, sibling relationships, competition, and rivalry.

Generally it is helpful to have the parent describe any sample of the child's problem-related behavior in the home environment. For instance, how does the eighth grade boy who is an underachiever approach his homework? What are his interests after school, his recreational patterns, the extent of his television viewing, etc.?

Diagnosis and decision have to be made jointly by the parent and counselor, frequently with teacher involvement. The counselor has to act as facilitator who will later help the parent implement the decision. At this final stage, the child also has to be drawn into the consulting process and given an opportunity to participate in finalizing the planned course of action. The stronger the involvement of the parent and child, the more successful the outcomes.

CONSULTATION WITH ADMINISTRATORS

Administrators occasionally request a consultation regarding a student in their school or a client served by their agency. Such consultation does not differ from the client-centered teacher consultation, which was discussed earlier in this chapter.

If the client is a professional member of the staff, e.g. a teacher of the school or a member of the agency team, the process of such consultation, while similar to client-centered consultation in the real sense, involves an additional layer of responsibility. The consultant has to be concerned not only with the needs of the consultee and the client (a teacher or staff member), but also with the well-being of the consumers of the client's services (students or counselees). Because of these multiple concerns, the consultation process requires high levels of professional maturity and skills on the part of the consultant.

Consultee-centered consultation with administrators may at times grow out of a client-centered consultation or even out of a referral. For instance, a high school counselor is asked by the dean to help him cope with a rebellious male student who has been repeatedly disciplined in the dean's office. After discussing the case at some length, the counselor notices that the problem lies more with the dean, who tends to be too harsh, than with the offending boy. Obviously, much tact has to be applied in helping the dean understand his ineffective approach to helping the student. However, if the initial resistance of this administrator can be overcome, a significant improvement in his profesional functioning may result from the consultee-centered intervention.

In the majority of cases, consultee-centered interventions with administrators are tied with institutional consultations, to be covered in Chapter 11.

SUMMARY

1. Since counselors do most of their consulting work with teachers, parents of students, and administrators, it is important that they acquire adequate consultation skills for dealing with individuals.

2. All individual consultation can be either consultee-centered or client-centered, depending on the principal focus of the helping intervention.

3. A consultee-centered intervention with a teacher has been illustrated through an example. Particular emphasis has been placed on the interpersonal dynamics between consultant and consultee, on the use of the three helping strategies, and on the sequential development through the eight stages of consultation.

4. Special features of the client-centered consultation process have been explained in contrast with the consultee-centered intervention.

5. On the basis of the two consultation models, consulting work with parents has been explored, and its special characteristics have been identified.

6. Individual consultations with administrators are either client-centered, parallel to client-centered consultations with

teachers, or consultee-centered. Such consultee-centered interventions are usually interlinked with institutional consultations.

REFERENCES

*Brown, D., Wyne, M.D., Blackburn, J.E., and Powell, W.C.: *Consultation: Strategy for Improving Education.* Boston, Allyn and Bacon, 1979.

Canter, L., and Canter, M.: *Assertive Discipline: A Take Charge Approach for Today's Educator.* Los Angeles, Couter and Associates, 1976.

*Caplan, G.: *The Theory and Practice of Mental Health Consultation.* New York, Basic Books, 1970.

Carr, R.A.: The effects of preventive consultation with elementary school principals on changing teacher staff meeting behaviors. *Canadian Counselor, 10*:157-165, 1976.

Dreikurs, R., and Cassel, P.: *Discipline without Tears.* New York, Hawthorne, 1964.

Gumaer, J.: Educator's study selection and evaluation of outcome in school consultation. *Personnel and Guidance Journal, 59*:117-119, 1980.

Guydish, J.: Substance abuse and alphabet soup. *Personnel and Guidance Journal, 60*:397-401, 1982.

*Hollis, J.W., and Donn, P.A.: *Psychological Report Writing: Theory and Practice.* Muncie, IN, Accelerated Development, 1973.

Jason, L.A., Ferone, L., and Anderegg, T.: Evaluating ecological, behavioral, and process consultation interventions. *Journal of School Psychology, 17*: 103-115, 1979.

*Meyers, J.: Consultee-centered consultation with a teacher as a technique in behavior management. *American Journal of Community Psychology, 3*:111-121, 1975.

Meyers, J., Freidman, M.P., and Gaugham, E.J.: The effect of consultee-centered consultation on teacher behavior. *Psychology in the Schools, 12*:288-295, 1975.

Miles, J.H., and Hummel, D.L.: Consultant training in counselor education programs. *Counselor Education and Supervision, 19*:49-53, 1979.

Piersell, W.C., and Kratochwill, T.R.: Self-observation and behavior change: applications to academic and adjustment problems through behavioral consultation. *Journal of School Psychology, 17*:151-161, 1979.

Roe, A., and Siegelman, M.: *The Origin of Interests.* Washington, APGA, 1964.

Sonstegard, M.: A rationale for interviewing parents. *School Counselor, 12*: 72-76, 1964.

---

*Recommended readings

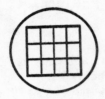

CHAPTER 7

SUPERVISION OF COUNSELORS
IN TRAINING

THIS chapter deals with the supervision of counselors during their field experiences, such as during counseling practicum and internships. As has been explained in Chapter 4, supervision encompasses the functions of several helping activities, in particular consultation, teaching, counseling, and evaluation. These activities are used concurrently, most of them in an intermittent pattern (*see* Figure 4-2).

In terms of the Three-Dimensional Intervention Model, individual supervision processes of counselor trainees are spread over the block of cells, 1 – A, B, C – I, II, III, as shown in Figure 7-1. Issue D, organizational structure and goals, rarely arises, unless there is institutional interference with the smooth operation of the students' field experiences or with their supervision. Consultee-centered consultation or teaching covers cells 1 – B – I, II, III; client-centered consultation, cells 1 – C – I, II, III; and counseling, cells 1 – A, B – I, II, III. Evaluation is concentrated in cells 1 – B – II, III, when concerned with counselor functioning, and in cells 1 – C – II, III, when focusing on the client's progress.

THE COUNSELING PRACTITIONER AS SUPERVISOR

How do counseling practitioners become involved in supervisory activities? Some of them are asked to cosupervise with

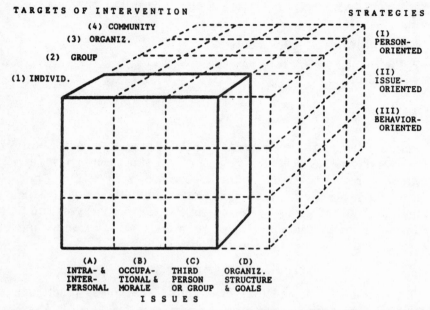

TARGETS OF INTERVENTION　　　　　　　　　　STRATEGIES

(4) COMMUNITY

(3) ORGANIZ.

(2) GROUP

(1) INDIVID.

(I)
PERSON-
ORIENTED

(II)
ISSUE-
ORIENTED

(III)
BEHAVIOR-
ORIENTED

(A)	(B)	(C)	(D)
INTRA- &	OCCUPA-	THIRD	ORGANIZ.
INTER-	TIONAL &	PERSON	STRUCTURE
PERSONAL	MORALE	OR GROUP	& GOALS

I S S U E S

Figure 7-1. Perimeter of Individual Supervision of Counselors in Training (Solid Lines) within the Three-Dimensional Intervention Model (Dotted Lines).

college instructors counselor education students whose practicum or internship experiences have been scheduled in schools or agencies where the counselors work. Also, the more experienced counselors supervise – as part of their jobs – newly hired staff members who have only recently entered the professional field. Such supervisory tasks can be professionally and personally enriching events, even for experienced counselors. Unfortunately, many practitioners view such opportunities for enrichment with mixed feelings, partly because of the additional work, but especially because their supervisory role has not been well defined.

To derive optimal benefits from supervisory tasks, counselors need a set of clear, explicit, and theoretically sound guidelines that would form the basis for a workable supervision model. Such a model has to be sufficiently flexible to integrate the predominant approaches to supervision. It is proposed here and explained in terms of —

1. Major historical antecedents
2. Envisioned supervisory processes
3. Practical applications

HISTORICAL ANTECEDENTS

During the past two decades, the role of practicum and internship supervisors has been the subject of ongoing discussions. One group of professionals identified supervision with teaching and concentrated heavily on the acquisition of counseling skills by the students. Another group perceived supervision primarily as counseling with the envisioned goal of promoting self-awareness and personality development of the supervisees.

The Teaching Approach

Walz and Roeber (1962) have found that most practicum supervisors perceived themselves primarily as teachers. It is accurate to state that this didactic approach to supervision has been prevalent, not only among counselor educators (Lambert, 1974), but also among other clinical supervisors (Kadushin, 1974; Haley, 1977). Even the ACES standards for counselor preparation seem to have favored the didactic approach, at least in their wording: "The practicum and internship experiences are tutorial forms of instruction" (ACES, 1973, Section II, C, 3, c).

In terms of theoretical foundations, the teaching approach to supervision has been heterogeneous. It included not only behavioral and cognitive orientations, but also process-oriented and personal-emotive strategies. Its unifying principle was the argument that students should use their clinical training experiences for translating theoretical knowledge into therapeutic skills.

Behavioral theorists, e.g. Krumboltz (1967) and Lazarus (1968), defined counseling as the process of changing clients' behaviors through imitative and operant learning in the cognitive and emotive domains. They perceived supervision in parallel terms, as "changing the behavior of behavior changers" — an opportunity for trainees to acquire skills for identifying clients' problems and for designing appropriate learning processes.

The cognitive orientation was represented by the Adlerian school. Dreikurs and Sonstegard (1966) promoted a group approach to teaching counseling skills. The supervisor acted as a directive group leader of perhaps a dozen trainees and instructed them in interviewing sequences that focused particularly on the mistaken goals of clients and the interpretation of such goals. The use of interviewing skills was to be demonstrated by individual trainees in front of the group, with peer feedback and supervisor critique to follow.

Other cognitively oriented supervision models emerged in the 1970s in response to the calls for accountability, particularly in educational settings. Aubrey (1978) presented a broad competency-based supervision program with an extensive list of skills ranging from individual and group counseling to coordinating school and community resources as its goals. Ivey and Authier (1978) provided a taxonomy of counseling skills that combined Rogerian constructs with elements of other theories. They have devised a laboratory training model based on behavioral methodology while at the same time emphasizing attitudinal learning. Martin, Hiebert, and Marx (1981) proposed a supervision model largely based on the discipline of instructional psychology.

Research has generally supported the validity of the teaching orientation in practicum supervision. Birk (1972) and Cormier and Hackney and Segrist (1974) found the didactic model of supervision to be highly effective by itself, while Goldfarb (1978) arrived at a parallel conclusion when evaluating the use of the didactic model in combination with other supervisory styles.

The Counseling Approach

An article by Arbuckle (1963) on the learning of counseling was historically significant for its advocacy of a counseling model of supervision (Brammer and Wassmer, 1977; Gurk and Wicas, 1979). Although by our present standards the article was moderate in its content and tone, it stirred up the professional community when published and generated a lively discussion in the years that followed (*cf.* Patterson, 1964).

Concurrently, the Rogerian emphasis on facilitating personal growth through supervision was underscored by Carkhuff and Berenson (1967), who pointed to the similarity of dynamics in supervision and therapy. To facilitate growth, both supervisors and counselors had to communicate empathy, warmth, and genuineness. Carkhuff (1968) placed particular emphasis on helping trainees develop trust in their experiences. Perrone and Sanborn (1966) perceived practicum as an apprenticeship that should promote the overall personal development of the learner, and Harmon (1977) considered the trainee's self-discovery and expanding self-awareness to be the principal goals of supervision.

The task of translating the theoretical postulates into operational processes was undertaken by Kagan (1972, 1975). His interpersonal process recall (IPR) was meant to recreate the existential context of the trainee's counseling encounter and to promote awareness and understanding of the dynamics involved in it. Some of the cues missed or misinterpreted would come to light and the therapeutic encounter would assume a greater experiential depth. The IPR method has been modified in various ways, e.g. by Gimmestad and Greenwood (1974), who applied it to work with *groups* of practicum students. It was also incorporated into other supervision models, e.g. the psychobehavioral supervision process (Boyd, 1978).

The counseling-oriented school of supervision has shown little interest in teaching particular techniques or specific counselor responses. Its top priorities have been the trainee's sensitivity, authentic self-experiencing, and ultimately, self-enhancement.

The Integrative Approach

Although the two contrasting views of supervision, the teaching and the counseling approach, are often expressed with considerable force, they do not reflect a true dichotomy. The gap between them is not insurmountable, for they represent differences in emphasis rather than in principle. It is well to remember that in the practice of helping professions, doctrinaire approaches are usually counterproductive. Brammer and Wassmer (1977) observe that theoretically puristic supervision, exclusively committed to a particular orientation, "occurs very rarely in the real world of counselor education. When it does, . . . the supervisor in question is probably more devoted to the system of supervision than to the real educational needs of his trainees" (p. 80).

The new, integrative approach to supervision has grown out of the realities of clinical training that is becoming increasingly eclectic. Most supervisors do not adhere to any single model but combine a variety of approaches. Leddig and Bernard (1980) believe that after an amorphous stage and a stage of polarization, supervision is assuming a *collaborative* format that emphasizes the learning of skills and the approach of cognitive psychology. Gurk and Wicas (1979) present an inclusive supervision model and place it within the framework of consultation. In their view, this "metamodel" can accommodate both the teaching and the counseling emphasis and any other gray areas of supervision.

Such an integrative supervision model, primarily involving consultation, is also proposed in this volume. It presents supervision as a collaborative enterprise that implies shared goal setting, problem solving, exploration of counseling strategies, and evaluation of counseling outcomes by supervisor and trainee (Kurpius and Baker, 1977). The integrative supervision model complies with the standards set by Patterson (1964): (1) Supervision is not therapy; (2) supervision must have a therapeutic climate; and (3) supervision has to provide learning experiences for students.

SUPERVISORY PROCESSES

As explained earlier in this chapter, supervision incorporates the helping processes of counseling and consultation, and within consultation, the functions of teaching, problem solving, and evaluation. These processes and functions tend to overlap as they are used in response to the needs of the trainee.

In chronological sequence, counseling may be used in the early stages of supervision and again at some later point. However, consultation provides the overall structure (1) in its consultee (trainee)-centered format, as teaching and evaluation of the trainee, and (2) in its client-centered format, as problem solving for the benefit of the client and as evaluation of the client's progress. In the early stages of supervision, trainee-centered consultation (teaching) is predominant. As the trainee becomes more self-directive and his or her skills improve, the format of consultation shifts to client-centered, focusing primarily on the problem and progress of the client.

Counseling

During the rapport-building stage, the supervisor concentrates on the subjective world of the trainee. The use of the person-oriented strategy at times triggers an emotional reaction in the trainee, who may reach out for help to deal with unresolved personal problems. The following question arises: When and to what extent should the supervisor act as counselor for the trainee?

Two situations come to mind in which counseling by the supervisor is *not* in the best interest of the trainee. One is when the supervisor obviously lacks the necessary time to provide adequate counseling. Another is when the trainee seems to have ulterior aims, e.g. trying to avoid the full impact of the clinical experience by bringing up personal problems during supervisory sessions. Kadushin (1968) warns that some trainees play games, one of them being "Protect the Sick and Infirm."

However, there are legitimate instances in which short-term personal counseling by the supervisor is appropriate. The trainee may need to solve an acute personal problem or cope with an adverse situation that has emerged in the course of professional training or is related to his or her career plans. This may involve marriage problems triggered by the pressure of graduate study or internal conflicts, e.g. in a female trainee who has a strong need for professional involvement but feels guilty about neglecting her children. In such situations the supervisor should offer short-term personal counseling, provided that (1) the request was made or implied by the trainee (prying into personal affairs of the trainee is never professionally acceptable) and (2) the supervisor and trainee can work out a sufficient time frame to accommodate personal counseling without limiting other functions of supervision.

Another instance where counseling is needed and should be initiated, even without the trainee's request, occurs when the supervisor becomes convinced that unresolved personal problems directly interfere with the trainee's counseling effectiveness. However, in this case it is advisable to offer the trainee a choice of various counseling opportunities, such as by referral to an outside therapist.

Counseling that needs to be done by supervisors should preferably be done in a short term. The ethical standards of the American Personnel and Guidance Association explicitly state their opposition to indiscriminate counseling of students by their supervisors: "When the education program offers a growth experience with an emphasis on self-disclosure or other relatively intimate or personal involvement, the member must have no administrative, supervisory, or evaluating authority regarding the participant" (APGA, 1981, Section H, 12).

A parallel view is held by writers in the field of counselor education (Cormier and Bernard, 1982) and in other helping professions, e.g. in psychiatry and social work. Ekstein and Wallerstein (1972), discussing supervision of psychiatric residents, observe that although both supervision and psychotherapy are interpersonal helping processes, "there is an essential difference between them created by the difference in purpose" (p. 254).

Trainee-Centered Consultation: Teaching

The teaching process in supervision covers both counseling attitudes and skills of the trainee. Its approach is similar to the teacher-centered consultation discussed in the previous chapter. In terms of didactic models, it is personalized and interactional. "Learning results from the interaction *between the teacher and the student*, between student and his content, and between his thought and his life" (Lapp, Bender, Ellenwood, and John, 1975, p. 195).

Most supervisory teaching occurs through role modeling (living one's role, not merely playing it). Senour (1982) points out the great influencing power of modeling, which is additionally augmented by the degree of genuineness in the role model (Corey, 1977). Particularly in the area of attitudinal learning, modeling has been shown to be more effective than the use of feedback linked with praise or criticism (Gulanick and Schmeck, 1977). While the supervisor serves as personal role model for the trainee, the quality of their mutual relationship (Buber, 1970; Rogers, 1961) greatly influences the trainee's relationships with clients.

Field experiences are the culmination of the student's graduate program. By the time counseling practicum or internship begins, the systematic instructional sequence should have been completed. The supervisor may assume that the trainee has mastered basic counseling skills and attitudes. *Teaching* in the context of supervision means helping the trainee translate theory into practice. It focuses on sharpening the previously acquired skills and on deepening the counseling attitudes.

However, there may be concepts or distinctions that need to be clarified for the trainee. For instance, I have found that some practicum students do not fully understand the distinction between unconditional positive regard for the client as a person and the need for an objective, evaluative perspective on the client's behavior (separating the behaver from his or her behavior). If this distinction is not clear in the mind of the novice counselor, he or she may unwittingly reinforce counterproductive or antisocial behavior of the client.

The supervisor must be alert to such lack of conceptual clarity and remedy it in the process of supervision. If problems persist or the trainee shows some basic deficiency in knowledge, the supervisor should provide him or her with a structured learning module that would involve readings, skill-building exercises, and self-evaluation (Cormier and Cormier, 1976). The trainee-centered teaching function is part of the supervision process from beginning to end. However, the input of the supervisor diminishes in the later stages.

Trainee-Centered Consultation: Evaluation

In contrast to rapport building, when the supervisor concentrated primarily on the trainee's intrapersonal dynamics, the focus of trainee-centered consultation is broader; it concentrates on the trainee's total therapeutic behavior. This is particularly true in the case of evaluation, which is an objective assessment of the trainee's level of performance.

However, evaluation should not be based solely on the personal judgment of the supervisor. The trainee should always participate in the evaluation process (Moses and Hardin, 1978), particularly since self-generated performance feedback has been found equally effective as expert evaluation (Robinson, Kurpius, and Froehle, 1979). This collaborative approach to evaluation is inherent in the concept of process consultation (Schein, 1978), which was discussed in Chapter 4.

In my view, the evaluation process should be geared toward stimulating professional growth in the trainee and not perceived as a threat. Therefore, primary emphasis should be placed on the positive accomplishments of the trainee and on the successes in counseling, although the trainee's weaknesses must not be glossed over. At times, when little improvement has occurred in the client's behavior, the reason for this apparent failure may not lie in the trainee's performance but in external circumstances.

A meaningful evaluation of the trainee's performance cannot occur unless the supervisor and trainee have agreed at the beginning of the supervision process on a mutually acceptable *contract*. It is a statement of concrete objectives that should include minimal counselor competencies that are mandated by the institution or selected from the list of counseling skills and the trainee's personally chosen goals.

The process of evaluation is an honest attempt to compare the planned final objectives stated in the contract with the actual achievement at various stages of the field experience. At the beginning, even minor progress is to be considered satisfactory. At later stages, the performance level of the trainee should move progressively closer to the final objectives spelled out in the contract. For the purpose of assessing the gradual progress of the trainee, it is useful to keep two or three early counseling tapes and compare them with more advanced tapes at later stages. Some supervisors use typescripts of the trainee's counseling sessions for that purpose.

Although evaluation in field experiences focuses primarily on the counseling process, it should not overlook other important areas of counselor functioning, such as report writing, professional cooperation, proficiency in referral procedures, and a general ability to structure and organize one's professional activities.

Client-Centered Consultation in Supervision

The triadic nature of supervision, involving client, trainee, and supervisor, is particularly evident when the supervisory process focuses on the problems and the therapeutic progress of the client. Along with the initial emphasis on improving the trainee's skills, the person and the social environment of the client take center stage of supervision.

All helping interventions involve diagnosis, treatment, and evaluation of outcomes. A clear classification system of problems found in clients is a major diagnostic aid for a novice counselor. Callis (1965) offers such a taxonomy based on (1) the areas of concern (vocational, emotional, and educational) and (2) the causes of problems (lack of self-understanding, lack of information about one's environment, conflict within self, conflict with significant others, and lack of skills). By this method, every problem can be identified (e.g. emotional — lack of self-understanding), and the diagnostic process assumes greater clarity. However, the trainee must be warned against the danger of oversimplifying complex human issues, a danger inherent in all taxonomies.

Following the diagnosis, the therapeutic intervention is planned. Although the trainee may have acquired a preferred approach, the nature of the client's problem may require a particular therapeutic emphasis (*cf.* the three strategies of intervention discussed in Chapter 5). In the process of the intervention, the therapeutic emphasis may have to be adjusted again and again to meet the needs of the client. Eventually, the outcomes of counseling are assessed in terms of the client's ability to cope, make responsible decisions, etc.

Table 7-I presents an overview of the helping processes involved in the overall course of supervision. How these processes are applied at the various stages of supervision will be explained in the following section.

TABLE 7-I

HELPING PROCESSES INVOLVED IN SUPERVISION

(1) SHORT-TERM COUNSELING FOR TRAINEE

    (Counseling offered when needed and under the con-
ditions discussed in this chapter. Even if no counseling is offered, a therapeutic climate has to be
maintained throughout the supervision process.)

(2) TRAINEE-CENTERED CONSULTATION

    (a) Contract: setting of goals

    (b) Teaching: applying theory to practice

        * deepening of professional attitudes

        * sharpening of counseling skills

    (c) Evaluation of trainee's counseling performance

(3) CLIENT-CENTERED CONSULTATION

    (a) Diagnosis of the client's problem

    (b) Treatment provided for the client

    (c) Evaluation of the outcomes of counseling

        for the client

PRACTICAL APPLICATIONS

First Stage of Supervision: Entry, Rapport Building

Before entering into a supervisory relationship, the counselor
has to ask some important questions: "Am I ready for a supervisory job? Do I have enough experience? Do I feel competent to
accept the simultaneous responsibility for the trainee's professional growth and for the welfare of the clients who will be under
his or her care?" Once the counselor feels ready for the task, he or
she should accept the supervisory role as a new challenge.

Tandem Supervision

When the supervisory project requires sharing responsibility with a faculty member (tandem supervision), such as in the case of practicum or internship supervision, the counselor should meet with the faculty person before the supervision commences. The two of them need to develop rapport and to make concrete plans for the supervision project. It should be clarified who does what, when, and how often. Also, the degree of ultimate responsibility that the faculty member and the counselor will assume must be spelled out. The tandem supervisors should keep in contact throughout the entire supervision project.

Another important point is to specify the goals or objectives of the practicum or internship project. In most cases the faculty member will provide the supervising counselor with a syllabus and with a practicum or internship manual, which explain the objectives and requirements of the field experience (*cf.* Dimick and Krause, 1975). Parenthetically, it should be added that tandem supervision is similar to dual supervision in which a faculty member and an advanced graduate student jointly supervise a practicum trainee. However, the advanced graduate student operates under supervision of the faculty person (Davis and Arvey, 1978).

If no faculty member is involved in the supervision, and the counseling practitioner assumes full responsibility for the project, it is still useful to obtain clarification of institutional expectations and of final evaluation criteria.

Rapport with the Trainee

The counselor needs to meet with the trainee at the earliest opportunity, primarily for the purpose of rapport building. The quality of the relationship between supervisor and trainee is of crucial importance for the success of supervision. During the initial meeting, the counselor should focus on the needs and concerns of the trainee and counteract any anxiety triggered by anticipation of the clinical experience. As has been mentioned earlier, the genuineness of the supervisor-trainee relationship will serve as a model for the trainee-client relationship. In the process of supervision, the relationship should develop into a professional partnership marked by mutual respect and caring.

The supervisor may want to know whether the trainee prefers a particular counseling approach and whether he or she has certain professional interests and priorities. Most supervisors disclose, at least indirectly, their own counseling orientation and personal values during this informal shop talk. However, they must carefully avoid *imposing* their counseling orientation or personal values on the trainees. True professionals are honest in expressing their views while allowing the trainees the full freedom to chart their own lives and careers. Matching supervisors and trainees on the basis of similar values is not necessary for a satisfactory relationship or a good quality of communication (Lemons and Lanning, 1979).

Planning the Project

Along with rapport building, the supervisor needs to acquaint the trainee with the technical requirements of the field experience (e.g. providing an audio recorder and tapes), with the required forms to be used (permission for taping, log, reports, etc.), and with the physical plant of the school or agency where the experience will take place. The trainee also needs to become aware of the educational or therapeutic goals of the host institution and of the special needs of its client population.

At this point the supervisor should assign the trainee homework: "Make a list of objectives you want to achieve by this clinical experience. Which skills and competencies do you want to master? Which counseling attitudes do you wish to expand and solidify?" By the end of the initial meeting, the supervisor introduces the trainee to the administrator and to staff members of the school or agency.

A tentative schedule for practicum or internship experiences is to be drawn up. The supervisor needs to make sure that an appropriate cross section of clients will be available to the trainee. At first, less complicated cases should be handled to give the trainee a chance to experience success. More difficult clients should be added later, at least four or five of them, for more extensive counseling, lasting perhaps five to six weeks. Internship experiences should additionally include other professional activities performed by counselors of the host institution.

Second Stage of Supervision: Beginning Consultation — Goal Setting, Teaching

As in every consultation, the relationship between the consulting supervisor and trainee is a partnership (Schein, 1978). The supervisor as senior partner should structure the relationship as a staff (rather than line) interaction, in a democratic, cooperative fashion.

Either prior to the first supervisory session or as part of it, the supervisor and the trainee should finalize the goals of the clinical experience. The informal contract should include objectives required by the institution and those chosen by the trainee. Having discussed and finalized the contract, the supervisor and trainee may want to make a few written or mental notes for future reference.

The Weekly Supervisory Meetings

Such meetings always involve sharing audiotape or videotape samples of the week's interviews. Another useful technique is to observe the trainee's counseling work through a one-way vision glass and to present a critique immediately afterward. There is a variety of models for analyzing the counseling process, such as IPR (Kagan, 1972), microtraining (Ivey and Simek-Downing, 1980), and unstructured psychotherapeutic supervision (Boyd, 1977). The supervisor should select one or a combination of models, according to his or her preference. The approach presented here incorporates elements of various methods.

I usually start with a brief rapport "refresher" and focus on the trainee and his or her verbal and nonverbal communication with me, e.g. I say "How was your week? Any particular event that was highly satisfying or traumatic? How did you feel about yourself as a practicing counselor?" Open-ended questions should be asked whenever possible to explore the current frame of mind of the trainee.

I then switch to the issue-oriented strategy and ask for information on the client whose tape will be played. (If I have already previewed the tape, the data would have been presented to me on a slip of paper along with the tape.) This includes age; sex; family situation of the client; if in school, achievement level; and the nature of the apparent problem. I also ask that the trainee summarize in two or three sentences what has happened in the counseling interveiw.

After that, we listen to the tape. I stop the tape periodically and ask how the trainee feels about the preceding verbal exchange with the client: "What do you think the client was telling you? How did you feel about it at the time?" We compare our perceptions of the feelings the client seemed to communicate. Although consensus of supervisor and trainee is not necessary, the comparison provides a clarification of what actually has happend.

I then focus on the trainee's therapeutic messages: "How do you feel about what you said to the client? Did you have a particular intention or goal in mind?" I try to point out the helpful elements of the counselor's communication first. Then I mention some of the less effective statements, and we explore what other approaches may work better. As we progress through the semester, I encourage self-critique by the trainee and decrease my own input.

Typical Problems Encountered

One of the most frequent problems that supervisors have to deal with in the beginning stages of supervision is the trainee's inability to tolerate silence and his or her tendency to speak too quickly. This makes it difficult for clients to be aware of and to open up to their own feelings. I always assure my trainees that these two deficiencies, which are typical of novice counselors, can be overcome with effort and practice. I try to impress upon them the need to focus their full attention on the client — on the client's total self-expression.

The client's cognitive messages are not easily ignored. However, it is relatively easy to miss their emotional connotations. The supervisor must make every effort to help the trainee "listen with the third ear" (Reik, 1949), become attuned to the client's inner process, and eventually be able to "walk in the client's moccasins." It is at this point that the trainee realizes how draining the work of the counselor can be, since it "requires a kind of alertness and sensitivity that are called for in few other types of human activity" (Tyler, 1969, p. 52).

Skills to Promote

The supervisory experience provides excellent opportunities to sharpen the counseling skills of the trainee. Particular attention should be given to the following skill areas:

1. Reflecting content and feelings
2. Asking open-ended questions (that cannot be answered by "yes" or "no")
3. Using minimal encouragers (nodding, saying, "So. . .?", "Well. . .?", or "Something else. . .?")
4. Clarification of statements ("Do I understand you correctly that. . .?")
5. Tentative interpretation ("Perhaps you did it because. . . .")
6. Encouragement ("That must make you feel good.")
7. Nonverbal skills, particularly involving eye contact and the interpretation of vocal cues (voice quality) and body language, in addition to the spoken words (Wilbur and Wilbur, 1980)
8. Skills for starting an interview (facilitate transition from small talk to a counseling encounter) and for ending an interview (help client maintain momentum of the therapeutic growth process beyond the interview)

Third Stage of Supervision: Ongoing Consultation — Problem Solving

The trainee and I discuss the overall quality of the counseling relationship from our two respective viewpoints and focus on the world of the client. In which general category does the client's problem fall (*see* p. 106, taxonomy by Callis, 1965)? Is it primarily self-generated or environmentally induced? We discuss the symptoms, the milieu in which the client lives, influences of significant others, etc. and eventually agree on a tentative diagnosis.

As the problem-solving approach continues, we try to identify the goals of the counseling intervention, to decide on a therapeutic approach that seems most appropriate, and to determine whether any psychological testing is needed. I impress upon my trainees their responsibility for *structuring* the counseling process. This involves developing a sound, collaborative counselor-client perspective on long-term and short-term objectives (Day and Sparacio, 1980). Without structuring, the counseling process will turn into "aimless interviewing" that produces few positive results (Tyler, 1969). I always ask my trainees to make concrete, yet flexible, plans for the next interview with each of their clients.

It is a sign of progress when the trainee takes personal initiative in structuring the counseling process. If this initiative is lacking, the supervisor must gently but firmly press the trainee to assume more responsibility for the counseling process. It is in the nature of effective supervision that it helps the trainee progress through a professional maturation process to self-supervision (Littrell, Lee-Borden, and Lorenz, 1979).

The individual supervision sessions are typically supplemented by weekly group meetings attended by all practicum or internship participants. Such meetings are usually supervised by the faculty person. If the counseling practitioner has to assume responsibility for the group meetings, he or she should structure them much like staff conferences (to be discussed in Chapter 9).

Fourth Stage of Supervision: Evaluation

As has been mentioned earlier, evaluation of the trainee's performance is an act of comparing his or her current performance with the stated objectives contained in the supervision contract. In my experience, it is useful to have a brief evaluation of progress at the end of each supervisory meeting or at least every two weeks. Such periodic evaluations are meant to challenge the trainee's motivation and to offer encouragement by recognizing his or her effort and progress. If deficiencies are pointed out, it should be done in a supportive way: "Let's see how you can best overcome this problem...."

For the final evaluation, a one-hour period should be reserved. The objectives of the field experience need to be reviewed one by one. Also, the quality of the trainee's written reports, the accuracy of data in the log, and the degree of cooperation with other professionals, particularly at staff meetings, should be assessed.

In the spirit of process consultation, the supervisor should impress upon the trainee that the field experience has been only the

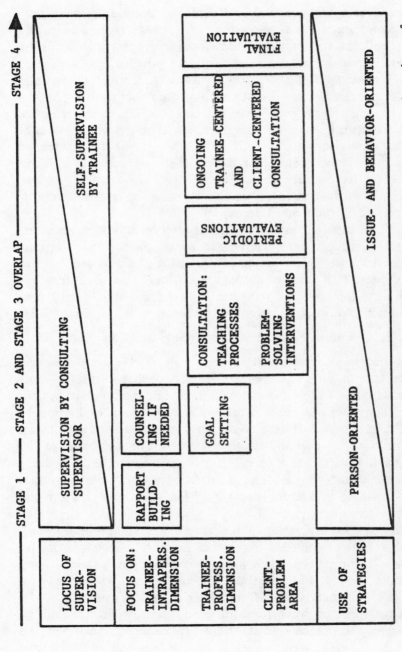

Figure 7-2. The Overall Process of Supervision According to Stages. The top section refers to the primary locus of responsibility for supervision. The midsection refers to the foci of supervision at any given stage (trainee- or client-centered). The lower section refers to the primary strategies to be used throughout the process.

beginning of a lifelong learning process that is an ongoing challenge for every true professional.

Figure 7-2 offers a graphic representation of the overall course of supervision and shows how the various helping processes are applied in the sequence of supervision stages.

SUMMARY

1. Counseling practitioners who occasionally supervise counselor trainees need clear guidelines for their supervisory task. Supervision becomes then a professionally enriching experience.

2. In theory, supervision is being perceived either as a teaching or as a counseling function. However, in practice, these models often merge within an eclectic methodology.

3. An integrative approach to supervision, based on the model of process consultation, has been presented here. This approach is broad enough to accommodate both the teaching and the counseling models.

4. The integrative consultation model involves various functions that are applied concurrently or intermittently, such as counseling, trainee-centered consultation (teaching and evaluation), and client-centered consultation.

5. Practical applications of these theoretical assumptions have been explored, and stages of the supervisory process have been identified. Special attention has been given to the structure of the weekly supervisory meetings.

6. The process of supervision should lead to the development of self-directiveness in the client who may have entered the clinical experience with a high degree of dependency.

REFERENCES

ACES: Standards for the preparation of counselors and other personnel services specialists. Washington, ACES, 1973 (mimeographed).

APGA: Ethical standards. *Guidepost* (supplement), 1981.

Arbuckle, D.S.: The learning of counseling: Process, not product. *Journal of Counseling Psychology, 10*: 163-167, 1963.

Aubrey, R.F.: Supervision of counselors in elementary and secondary schools. In Boyd, J. (Ed.): *Counselor Supervision: Approaches, Preparation, Practices.* Muncie, IN, Accelerated Development, 1978, pp. 293-338.

Birk, J.M.: Effects of counseling supervision method and preference on empathic understanding. *Journal of Counseling Psychology, 19*:542-546, 1972.

*Boyd, J.: *Counselor Supervision: Approaches, Preparation, Practices,* Muncie, IN, Accelerated Development, 1978.

*Brammer, L.M., and Wassmer, A.C.: Supervision in counseling and psychotherapy. In Kurpius, D.J., Baker, R.D., and Thomas, I.D. (Eds.): *Supervision of Applied Training: A Comparative Review.* Westport, CT, Greenwood Press, 1977, pp. 43-87.

Buber, M.: *I and Thou.* New York, Scribner's, 1970.

*Callis, R.: Diagnostic classification as a research tool. *Journal of Counseling Psychology, 12*:238-247, 1965.

Carkhuff, R.R.: A "non-traditional" assessment of graduate education in the helping professions. *Counselor Education and Supervision, 7*: 252-261, 1968.

Carkhuff, R.R., and Berenson, B.G.: *Beyond Counseling and Psychotherapy.* New York, Holt, Rinehart and Winston, 1967.

Corey, G.: *Theory and Practice of Counseling and Psychotherapy.* Monterey, CA, Brooks-Cole, 1977.

Cormier, L.S., and Bernard, J.M.: Ethical and legal responsibilities of clinical supervisors. *Personnel and Guidance Journal, 60*:486-491, 1982.

Cormier, L.S., and Cormier, W.H.: Developing and implementing self-instructional modules for counselor training. *Counselor Education and Supervision, 16*:37-45, 1976.

*Cormier, L.S., Hackney, H., and Segrist, A.: Three counselor training models: A comparative study. *Counselor Education and Supervision, 14*: 95-104, 1974.

*Davis, K.L., and Arvey, H.H.: Dual supervision: A model for counseling and supervision. *Counselor Education and Supervision, 17*:293-299, 1978.

Day, R.W., and Sparacio, R.T.: Structuring the counseling process. *Personnel and Guidance Journal, 59*:246-249, 1980.

*Dimick, K.M., and Krause, F.H.: *Practicum Manual for Counseling and Psychotherapy.* Muncie, IN, Accelerated Development, 1975.

Dreikurs, R., and Sonstegard, M.A.: A specific approach to practicum supervision. *Counselor Education and Supervision, 6*:18-25, 1966.

Ekstein, R., and Wallerstein, R.S.: *The Teaching and Learning of Psychotherapy,* 2nd ed. New York, International Universities Press, 1972.

Gimmestad, M.J., and Greenwood, J.D.: A new twist on IPR: Concurrent recall by supervisory group. *Counselor Education and Supervision, 14*:71-73, 1974.

Goldfarb, N.: Effects of supervisory style on counselor effectiveness and facilitative responding. *Journal of Counseling Psychology, 25*:454-460, 1978.

---

*Recommended readings

Gulanick, N., and Schmeck, R.R.: Modeling, praise, and criticism in teaching empathic responding. *Counselor Education and Supervision, 16*:284-290, 1977.

Gurk, M.D., and Wicas, E.A.: Generic models of counseling supervision: Counseling/instruction dichotomy and consultation metamodel. *Personnel and Guidance Journal, 57*:402-407, 1979.

Haley, J.: *Problem Solving Therapy.* San Francisco, Jossey-Bass, 1977.

Harmon, R.L.: Beyond techniques. *Counselor Education and Supervision, 17*: 157-158, 1977.

*Ivey, A.E., and Authier, J.: *Microcounseling: Innovations in Interviewing, Counseling, Psychotherapy, and Psychoeducation,* 2nd ed. Springfield, IL, Thomas, 1978.

Ivey, A.E., and Simek-Downing, L.: *Counseling and Psychotherapy: Skills, Theories, and Practice.* Englewood Cliffs, NJ, Prentice-Hall, 1980.

Kadushin, A.: Games people play in supervision. *Social Work, 13*:23-32, 1968.

*Kadushin, A.: Supervisor-supervisee: A survey. *Social Work, 19*:288-298, 1974.

*Kagan, N.: *Influencing Human Interaction.* East Lansing, MI, Michigan State University, 1972 (manual and films).

Kagan, N.: Influencing human interaction — eleven years with IPR. *Canadian Counselor, 9*:74-97, 1975.

Krumboltz, J.D.: Changing the behavior of behavior changers. *Counselor Education and Supervision, 6*:222-229, 1967.

Kurpius, D.J., and Baker, R.D.: The supervision process: Analysis and synthesis. In Kurpius, D.J., Baker, R.D., and Thomas, I.D. (Eds.): *Supervision of Applied Training.* Westport, CT, Greenwood, 1977.

Lambert, M.U.: Supervisory and counseling process: A comparative study. *Counselor Education and Supervision, 14*:54-60, 1974.

Lapp, D., Bender, H., Ellenwood, S., and John, M.: *Teaching and Learning: Philosophical, Psychological, Curricular Applications.* New York, Macmillan, 1975.

Lazarus, A.A.: The content of behavior therapy training. Paper presented at the meeting of the Association for the Advancement of Behavioral Therapies, San Francisco, 1968.

Leddig, G.R., and Bernard, J.M.: The history of supervision: A critical review. *Counselor Education and Supervision, 19*:186-196, 1980.

Lemons, S., and Lanning, W.E.: Value system similarity and the supervisory relationship. *Counselor Education and Supervision, 19*:13-19, 1979.

*Littrell, J.M., Lee-Borden, N., and Lorenz, J.R.: A developmental framework for counseling supervision. *Counselor Education and Supervision, 19*:129-136, 1979.

Martin, J., Hiebert, B.A., and Marx, R.W.: Instructional supervision in counselor training. *Counselor Education and Supervision, 20*:193-202, 1981.

_____
*Recommended readings

Moses, H.A., and Hardin, J.T.: A relationship approach to counselor supervision in agency settings. In Boyd, J. (Ed.): *Counselor Supervision: Approaches, Preparation, Practices.* Muncie, IN, Accelerated Development, 1978, pp. 441-480.

Patterson, C.H.: Supervising students in the counseling practicum. *Journal of Counseling Psychology, 11*:47-53, 1964.

Perrone, P.A., and Sanborn, M.P.: Early observation: An apprenticeship approach to counselor education. *Counselor Education and Supervision, 6*: 63-68, 1966.

Reik, T.: *Listening with the Third Ear.* New York, Farrar, Straus and Cadahy, 1949.

Robinson, S.E., Kurpius, D.J., and Froehle, T.C.: Self-generated performance feedback in the interviewing training. *Counselor Education and Supervision, 19*:91-100, 1979.

Rogers, C.R.: *On Becoming a Person.* Boston, Houghton Mifflin, 1961.

Schein, E.H.: The role of the consultant: Content expert or process facilitator? *Personnel and Guidance Journal, 56*:339-343, 1978.

Senour, M.N.: How counselors influence clients. *Personnel and Guidance Journal, 60*:345-349, 1982.

*Tyler, L.E.: *The Work of the Counselor,* 3rd ed. New York, Appleton-Century-Crofts, 1969.

Walz, G.R., and Roeber, E.C.: Supervisor's reaction to a counseling interview. *Counselor Education and Supervision, 2*:2-7, 1962.

Wilbur, M.P., and Wilbur, J.R.: Categories of nonverbal behavior: Implications for supervision. *Counselor Education and Supervision, 19*:197-209, 1980.

---

*Recommended reading

CHAPTER 8

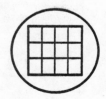

SUPERVISION OF COUNSELING
PRACTITIONERS

PROFESSIONAL literature makes a distinction between educational supervision of counselors in training and administrative supervision of counselors on the job (Kadushin, 1976; Downing and Maples, 1979). In the preceding chapter we have reviewed educational supervision of practicum and internship students, which on the Three-Dimensional Intervention Model covers the area 1 – A, B, C – I, II, III. The present chapter is devoted to administrative supervision of counseling practitioners in agency or school settings. In addition to issues A, B, and C, this also covers issue D, organizational structures and goals, as illustrated in Figure 8-1. Although administrative supervision borders on management, this chapter limits the subject to processes directly involving individual supervision.

UNDERSTANDING ADMINISTRATIVE SUPERVISION

Its Nature

Administrative supervision exceeds the scope of educational supervision in many ways. It contains all helping processes listed under educational supervision. (The caveat with regard to long-term counseling of supervisees by supervisors may be even more needed in the administrative context.) However, the functions of administrative supervision are broader. In addition to monitoring and evaluating individual performance, the administrative supervisor provides a professionally sound and personally satisfying work climate for the supervised counselors and promotes staff

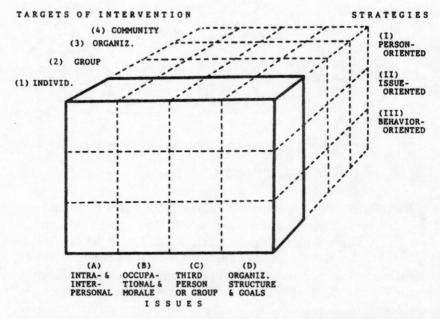

TARGETS OF INTERVENTION

(4) COMMUNITY
(3) ORGANIZ.
(2) GROUP
(1) INDIVID.

STRATEGIES

(I) PERSON-ORIENTED
(II) ISSUE-ORIENTED
(III) BEHAVIOR-ORIENTED

(A) INTRA- & INTER-PERSONAL
(B) OCCUPA-TIONAL & MORALE
(C) THIRD PERSON OR GROUP
(D) ORGANIZ. STRUCTURE & GOALS

ISSUES

Figure 8-1. Perimeter of Individual Supervision of Counseling Practitioners (Solid Lines) within the Three-Dimensional Intervention Model (Dotted Lines).

morale. Administrative supervision often extends to paraprofessional aides and secretarial support staff. It always includes some managerial functions, such as planning, implementing, and evaluating programs and acquiring adequate material resources to support them.

Elements of teaching and in-service training (consultee-centered consultation) are invariably present in administrative supervision, particularly for the benefit of novice counselors and paraprofessionals (Doyle, Foreman, and Wales, 1977). However, the supervision of professional staff members is largely program-related. It focuses on coordinating individual efforts toward the goals of the total program. While the success of educational supervision is assessed by the degree of counseling competence acquired by counselors in training, the success of administrative supervision is measured in terms of the overall functioning of a counseling agency or of a school guidance department.

Its Importance

Administrative supervision is of major importance for the profession. Its primary goals are intraprofessional: maintaining high standards of counseling work, monitoring the relevance of existing programs, and planning programmatic innovations in response to emerging client needs. Its secondary goals are in the area of professional visibility, related to the current demand for accountability in mental health and guidance work, particularly with regard to school settings (Carey and Garris, 1971; Lessinger, 1971; Crabbs and Crabbs, 1977). The public, which provides support for these programs, requires credible answers and accurate data as to which counseling and guidance activities are being offered and what good is being accomplished by the expenditure of appropriated funds. Unless the work of counselors is effectively monitored by supervisors who collect the data and communicate them to the public, the counseling profession may experience serious problems in the future (Downing and Maples, 1979).

Operational Patterns

Supervisors of mental health centers and other human services agencies are mostly professional counselors, therapists, or social workers who have come up through the ranks and have acquired an adequate understanding of the therapeutic work done by their colleagues. White (1981) considers it unusual to find a supervisor of a community mental health center who is not professionally trained and experienced in doing therapy. The author perceives this as an advantage, since experienced practitioners "are familiar with the type of services being provided and presumably know how to insure high quality service for the client and are best suited to orient and train new professionals who enter the organization" (p. 2).*

---

*From Steven L. White, *Managing Health and Human Services Programs, A Guide for Managers.* Reprinted by permission. Copyright © 1981. The Free Press, a division of Macmillan Publishing Co., Inc.

In contrast, administrative supervision of school counselors is usually assigned to persons who have no counseling background. The building principal is ordinarily the immediate supervisor of the guidance personnel of a school, while the county guidance director has only an indirect or consulting relationship with the counselors of the school district. In schools with several counselors, one of them usually serves as department head, who supervises the rest of the guidance staff and reports to the principal.

Some school systems have developed informal support structures for their guidance counselors. An example is the advisory council modality used in Hillsborough County, Florida.* Counselors at the elementary and junior high levels are typically the only guidance professionals in their schools. To maintain close contacts with their supervisor and among themselves, every year they elect representatives for a council that advises the county guidance supervisor. The council meets with the county supervisor monthly, and each council member meets with eight or nine counselors in his or her assigned group about five times a year. The structure provides upward and downward communication between the counselors in the field and the county supervisor and lateral communication among the counselors themselves. This system has been in existence for about ten years and has been well accepted by the counselors, by principals of the schools involved, and by the top administrators of the county school system. It is considered a viable complement to the official supervisory system mentioned above.

ADMINISTRATIVE SUPERVISION AS PROCESS CONSULTATION

As was mentioned earlier in this volume, supervision should not be an exercise in power, but rather a helping effort based on the principles of process consultation (Schein, 1969) that involves a partnership of supervisor and supervisee (Moses and Hardin, 1978). The supervisor should act as actualizer and facilitator of a developmental process in which the supervisee actively participates. Although their roles differ, supervisor and supervisee can share responsibility for outcomes of the supervision process.

---

*This information was provided by Joseph Greco, supervisor of guidance, Hillsborough County Schools, Tampa, Florida.

English, Oberle, and Byrne (1979) have found that counselors are highly responsive to a democratic, people-oriented supervision style, and Bennis (1966) considers democratic management a necessary condition of organizational vitality in an era of ongoing change.

People Orientation and Task Orientation

Kadushin (1976) summarizes several studies on the relative merits of interpersonal (people-oriented) supervision and technical (task- or product-oriented) supervision. He concludes that while the most effective supervisory model is achieved by an optimum mix of the two approaches, the human relations aspect is of major importance, even in organizations whose productivity depends primarily on machines. Obviously, human relations are substantially more important in organizations "in which the medium of service offered is the person of the worker herself. Machines do not have to feel a conviction in the work they are doing in order to do it well; they never suffer from depression, guilt, a sense of inadequacy. They are not jealous or envious of the achievements of other machines and do not feel competitive. They do not need to be inspired in order to work at an optimum level" (Kadushin, 1976, p. 200). This statement points out the cause-effect relationship that exists between worker-oriented supervision and worker enthusiasm, professional commitment, and staff morale.

Blake and Mouton (1978) contend that equally high levels of concern for people and for work efficiency complement each other and foster physical and mental health among workers in all settings. By placing appropriate emphasis on the quality of work and productivity, people-oriented supervisors promote professional self-esteem among the supervised counselors, who would rather be associated with a reputable organization than belong to a problem-ridden school or agency. Tolerating professional mediocrity on the counseling team is an insult to staff members and a sure way of destroying staff morale, usually resulting in the exodus of the best workers. Figure 8-2 shows the relationship of supervision priorities (people or task orientation) and leadership styles.

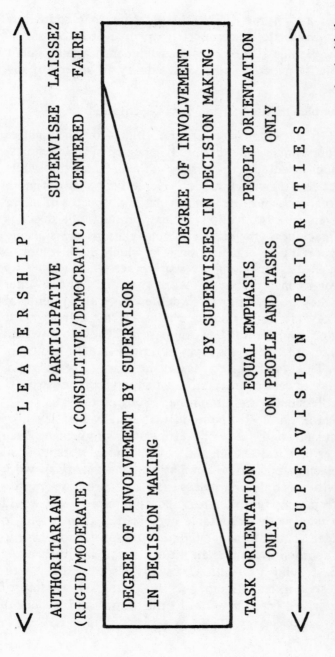

Figure 8–2. Leadership styles and supervision priorities can be perceived on two parallel continua, correlated with the degree of involvement in decision making by supervisor and supervisee.

Participatory Leadership

The supervision model proposed here is closely related to participatory democratic leadership (McGregor, 1960; Tannenbaum, Weschler, and Massarik, 1961; Halloran, 1978). As can be seen in Figure 8-2, this leadership model helps staff members become involved in decision making, e.g. about implementing the general policies of the institution. In this context, supervisors as midlevel administrators often have to serve as buffers between top management and the staff under their jurisdiction. They help adjust elements of the general policies to the needs of the consumers and bring them in line with available professional and technical resources.

When staff members are involved in planning operational processes, they should be able to express their views freely and with the knowledge that their input will receive due consideration (Goodstein, 1978). However, once the planning has been completed, the supervisor should assume full responsibility for carrying out the agreed-upon plan of action.

Staff members do not always have identical perceptions of the decisions that have been made. In such cases, the supervisor may have to assume the role of a catalyst and clarify the disputed issues, but must remain decisive in assuring that existing policies are carried out. Participatory leadership should not be confused with the laissez faire leadership model, and even less with weak and indecisive leadership.

The supervisor may, at times, be compelled to use his or her authority as a last resort for enforcing policies. In such cases, it is well to recall the admonition of Kadushin (1976) that the most effective use of authority is its minimal use. The supervisor has to resist the temptation to display power for its own sake. When forced to use the authority of his (her) office for overcoming an impasse, the supervisor should focus on issues rather than personalities, emphasize positive solutions rather than harp on the shortcomings of any person or group, and show that the use of authority is in the long-term interest of the supervisees. The more convicing the evidence that the supervisor's general intent is to serve rather than to control, the higher the level of his or her credibility in crisis situations.

Halloran (1978) emphasizes that supervisors who have been appointed and given authority are not always leaders: "All leaders have authority; but all authoritarians are not leaders. Leaders derive their authority *from* the group" (p. 298). It is highly desirable for an appointed supervisor to gain the approval of the group and combine formal supervisory authority with real leadership recognized by the group.

Communication

Since communication is a vital instrument for achieving mutual understanding among people, the supervisor must always keep open channels for two-way exchanges: vertical to the upper (or lower) echelons and lateral within the organizational team (Blake and Mouton, 1978). To deal effectively with staff members, the supervisor should be in personal touch with all of them — not with just a few favorites — and actively seek their input, both positive and critical. Giving people an opportunity to talk privately assures the supervisor of greater spontaneity of their expression than if all input is channeled exclusively through staff meetings, or even worse, through written reports.

When soliciting personal input from individuals, the supervisor must avoid irrelevant chitchat and gossip (Ekstein and Wallerstein, 1972). There need not be a dichotomy between a warm, acceptant attitude and a factual, professional emphasis of the supervisor who deals with staff members.

It is equally important that the supervisor keep all staff members well informed about developments that may affect them personally or professionally. This is particularly important in times of fiscal crises when cutbacks in counseling and guidance programs loom on the horizon. Staff members also have the right to know how the supervisor feels about their individual performance and what they can expect in terms of future employment and advancement. It is unprofessional when for months the supervisor remains silent about observed deficiencies of a staff member and points them out only during the annual evaluation.

If the supervisor has a policy of "leveling" with the staff, i.e. sharing relevant information and supplying accurate data, staff members gain a sense of personal involvement and identification with the organization, and they feel encouraged to make recommendations for improving its service (Blake and Mouton, 1978). They are also more agreeable to endure personal hardships due to budget cuts, particularly if they are convinced that this serves their long-term interest.

Clear Role Descriptions

One of the most unnerving conditions professional and paraprofessional workers have to endure is the lack of a clear description of their respective roles. In the extreme, this leads to chaos. In most cases it significantly lowers staff morale and generates interstaff conflicts (Aubrey, 1978). It may also produce burnout in well-motivated individuals due to role diffusion (Boy and Pine, 1980). As I have stated elsewhere (Drapela, 1979), whenever professional workers are teamed up with paraprofessionals, the cooperation is most successful if the respective areas of responsibility are clearly defined. Mitchell, Kantrowitz, and Davidson (1980) have arrived at a parallel conclusion with nonprofessionals who preferred well-defined roles to those that are loosely structured.

A clear job description should be provided as part of the orientation for all new staff members at the beginning of their employment. Supervisors prevent much dissatisfaction and loss of time and energy among their staff if they periodically clarify or revise the roles and functions of individual workers. By spelling out areas of responsibility they eliminate duplication of effort. In the spirit of process orientation, this should always be done with the involvement of the respective staff members. Boy and Pine (1980) suggest that attention be given to separating important tasks from trivial or meaningless functions and setting up priorities to meet client needs: "Counselors who have examined their roles and increased actual counseling time have moved toward greater involvement in the needs of their clients" (p. 163).

At times, there may be a conflict between the formal job description and the role perception of the counselor. This situation has to be handled with fairness and tact, and equal consideration should be given to the point of view of the counselor and to the rationale of the institution for its established policies. There may be a valid reason for adjusting policy to new circumstances identified by the counselor, in which case a change is in the best interest of the institution. However, if a policy is found to be well founded, a counselor who cannot accept it should resolve the conflict by leaving the institution. In the final analysis, the good of the clients to be served is the *ultimate* criterion for assessing the value of any policy.

PRACTICAL APPLICATIONS

By virtue of their position, supervisors have assumed a triple responsibility (1) toward the institution that provides the counseling services, (2) toward the clients who are consumers of the counseling services, and (3) toward the staff members who deliver the counseling services. Of the three, the responsibility toward staff members is the most important, since the quality of counseling hinges upon the performance of the staff.

The recommendations offered below are directly applicable to agency settings, but only indirectly to school settings, where guidance counselors are usually supervised by persons without a counseling background. Hopefully, the discussion will serve as stimulus for increased professionalization of the current supervisory system and in the meanwhile offer ideas for improving the various informal self-help programs organized by some school counselors.

Supervisors as Role Models

English, Oberle, and Byrne (1979) conducted a survey of counselors working in rehabilitation agencies to assess which personal characteristics they considered most desirable in their supervisors. According to this survey, which has implications for counselors in other fields, the most desirable characteristics were ranked as follows: (1) personal honesty, (2) leadership, (3) efficiency, and (4) concern for others. While both person-oriented traits and task-oriented traits are represented on this list, the concern for personal honesty of supervisors ranks first. It is not a smooth personal style, charm, political savvy, or social popularity but the supervisor's unquestionable honesty and concern for people that win loyalty, trust, and cooperation among supervisees. To model professional attitudes and to motivate staff members to high performance levels, supervisors have to be highly committed to their work. They should be willing "to walk the extra mile" whenever necessary for the good of their staff and clients and never ask of their supervisees what they are unwilling to undertake themselves.

Supervisors model their attitude of concern by serving as advocates of the rights of staff members both individually and collectively. This involves negotiating adequate salary levels and personnel benefits for all staff members with the top management and helping provide sufficient material resources for development of counseling programs.

One of the more difficult tasks supervisors must assume as part of their advocacy is arbitrating interpersonal or intergroup conflicts. This requires impartiality, sensitivity, and optimism. Roark (1978) offers useful suggestions for conflict management. The process generally involves reduction of conflict intensity, opening of communication, narrowing of ill-defined conflict issues to a central issue, and rediscovery of mutual respect, which eventually leads to conflict resolution. On a long-term basis, supervisors can serve as effective models of cooperative attitudes and thus counteract tendencies toward competition and jealousy among staff members.

A Balanced Supervision Approach

Effective supervisors have the good sense of avoiding either of the two extremes: (1) oversupervision, which communicates lack of trust and stifles self-directiveness of counselors and (2) undersupervision, which projects attitudes of disinterest or neglect and breeds professional stagnancy. The balanced approach is to provide supervision when needed, on a regular basis, and in a low-key fashion and to structure it as an assistance to staff members. This approach is consistent with the style used in process-consultation.

Counselor Activities to Be Supervised

Supervision of counselors on the job involves more than monitoring their counseling activities, although high quality counseling must always be the central emphasis. Activities that are to be supervised include the following:

1. *Counseling Activities*

   with individuals and small groups

2. *Guidance Activities*

   with large groups (particularly in school settings)

3. *Delivery of Information*

   educational (also to include data on scholarships, financial aids, etc.)

   vocational (a wide range of career opportunities; sex stereotyping in career planning to be avoided)

   personal-social (health issues, use of drugs and alcohol, social interaction skills, etc.)

4. *Assessment Procedures*

   standardized tests (their application and interpretation)

   nontest techniques (anecdotal reports, case studies, etc.)

5. *Consulting Activities*

   with teachers

   with parents

   with administrators

6. *Coordinating Activities*

   within school or agency (with administrators and among staff units)

   in the community (outreach programs)

A lengthier and more explicit list of the areas to be supervised, particularly in schools, has been presented by Aubrey (1978). In addition to the activities listed above, he includes research and writing, curriculum development and appraisal, and organizational and managerial efforts, each of these areas involving a number of competencies.

The Process of Supervision

The process of supervision typically moves through the stages explained in the previous chapter: rapport building, goal setting, problem solving, and evaluation.

Rapport Building and Goal Setting

When the supervisor and staff member establish sufficient rapport, they need to turn their attention to setting goals and negotiating a contract. An informal contract that spells out expected performance objectives and specifies how the individual's work would fit into the team effort should be negotiated with every staff member annually (Downing and Maples, 1979). While institutional goals should be given prominent attention, every individual counselor must have an opportunity to write into the contract his or her own objectives, such as counseling projects with particular client populations, peer counseling programs, etc., as long as they do not run contrary to the overall staff objectives. If such a contract is mutually agreed upon, the supervisor and counselor will have an easier task arriving at a summative evaluation at the end of the year.

Problem Solving through Consultation

As mentioned earlier, the supervision of counseling work is to be offered at regular intervals and structured as consultation. In agencies, the process can be arranged as follows:

A staff member conducting an individual or group counseling session is observed through a one-way vision glass or on videotape by the supervisor alone or in the company of several counselors. The supervisor and other involved counselors assume the role of consultants and focus primarily on the problems of the client (or group) and on the dynamics of the interaction. They discuss with the supervised counselor available options for dealing with the problems, explore alternatives, and stimulate solutions. This kind of supervision does not focus on the counselor's deficiencies, although it does not overlook them. It serves primarily as an opportunity for exchanging ideas that promote new insights and professional enrichment.

Evaluation

Scriven (1967) identifies two kinds of evaluation: (1) *formative* evaluation, which is used for raising the level of current performance, e.g. by suggesting new strategies or by employing untapped resources; and (2) *summative* evaluation, which is used for assessing the overall value of past performance in terms of generated effort, observed outcomes, cost-effectiveness, etc. The latter type of evaluation is used by supervisors as basis for contract renewals, salary increments, promotions, etc.

In applying these principles to evaluation of counseling practitioners, two points need to be made. First, summative evaluation, which occurs at a given point in time, should never be separated from the ongoing process of formative evaluation, carried out through observation, consultation, and long-term professional dialogue between supervisor and staff member.

Second, although all evaluation processes — summative and formative — are the responsibility of the supervisor, they should be handled as cooperative endeavors involving supervisor and staff member. As they have jointly negotiated a contract and agreed upon specific performance objectives, supervisor and staff member should assess together to what degree the objectives have been attained. Although senior by rank, the supervisor should view the staff member as a colleague rather than a subordinate and act accordingly. Pragmatic considerations recommend this approach as well. Unless the staff member is actively involved in identifying his or her strengths and weaknesses, it is questionable that any improvement of his or her professional work will occur.

In an atmosphere of mutual respect between supervisor and staff, evaluation procedures are not perceived as threatening. Instead, most staff members find them professionally refreshing. It is recommended that the supervisor occasionally volunteer to be observed and that his or her work be critiqued by others in order to serve as a role model for the staff.

Should staff members themselves become engaged in peer evaluation? Although this is still considered a controversial issue (Kadushin, 1976), peer involvement in formative evaluation through informal critique or mutual consultation seems appropriate. Provided that such an option exists, it is up to the staff members to decide as a group whether they wish to be involved in summative peer evaluation for the purpose of recommending individual members for continuing contract, salary increments, and promotions.

Supervision of Noncounseling Activities

As has been mentioned, supervisors are to monitor numerous other counselor activities besides counseling, such as testing programs, referral procedures, etc. This is done through reviewing mandatory written reports and through individual conferences with staff members. For purposes of documenting productivity of the agency or the school guidance staff, it is important that individual counselors keep a daily log of their activities, tabulate the data, and share the information with their supervisor on a regular basis.

The schedule of the individual supervisory activities and personal conferences has to be supplemented by weekly staff meetings, occasional group sessions, and in-service training projects throughout the year. The supervisor may wish to host occasional social gatherings, which can be great morale builders for the staff.

SUMMARY

1. Administrative supervision of counseling practitioners differs from educational supervision of counselors in training in several ways. Its scope is broader; it aims at promoting the overall effectiveness of counseling programs (rather than at teaching) and at communicating the outcomes of counselor work to the general public.

2. The proposed model of counselor supervision is based on process consultation in which a partnership between senior and junior professionals is emphasized. Although concerns for people take top priority, supervisors are to balance them with task orientation (1) to promote efficiency and (2) to foster self-esteem of staff members, since they prefer to be associated with reputable rather than mediocre institutions.

3. Participatory leadership, which helps supervisees participate in the decision-making process, and open communication — both vertical and lateral — are perceived as important components of the proposed supervisory model.

4. Supervisors have to provide a clear role description for every counselor on the staff. At times, there may be a conflict between the formal role description and the perception of the counselor. The supervisor has to help resolve such conflicts.

5. Supervisors are role models for their counselors. Attitudes and work patterns that they model have a major influence on the formation of the professional styles of their counselors.

6. Administrative supervision should be a nonthreatening process that includes both consultation and ongoing evaluation and is structured as a democratic interaction between supervisor and supervisee.

7. Administrative supervision of counselors has to cover not only counseling performance, but also other areas of professional counselor involvement.

REFERENCES

Aubrey, R.F.: Supervision of counselors in elementary and secondary schools. In Boyd, J. (Ed.): *Counselor Supervision: Approaches, Preparation, Practices.* Muncie, IN, Accelerated Development, 1978, pp. 293-338.

Bennis, W.: *Beyond Bureaucracy: Essays on the Development and Evolution of Human Organizations.* New York, McGraw-Hill, 1966.

Blake, R.R., and Mouton, J.S.: *The New Managerial Grid.* Houston, Gulf Publishing, 1978.

Boy, A.V., and Pine, G.J.: Avoiding counselor burnout through role renewal. *Personnel and Guidance Journal, 59*:161-163, 1980.

*Carey, A.R., and Garris, D.L.: Accountability for school counselors. *School Counselor, 18*:321-326, 1971.

Crabbs, S.K., and Crabbs, M.A.: Accountability: Who does what to whom, when, where, and how? *School Counselor, 25*:104-109, 1977.

*Downing, C.J., and Maples, M.I.: School counselor field supervision: A model. *Counselor Education and Supervision, 19*:153-160, 1979.

Doyle, W.W., Foreman, M.E., and Wales, E.: Effects of supervision in the training of nonprofessional crisis-intervention counselors. *Journal of Counseling Psychology, 24*:72-78, 1977.

---

*Recommended readings

Drapela, V.J.: Cooperation of various counseling services. Paper read at the Ninth World Congress of the International Association of Educational and Vocational Guidance, Konigstein, Germany, September 1979.

Ekstein, R., and Wallerstein, R.S.: *The Teaching and Learning of Psychotherapy*, 2nd ed. New York, International Universities Press, 1972.

*English, R.W., Oberle, J.B., and Byrne, A.R.: Rehabilitation counselor supervision: A national perspective. *Rehabilitation Counseling Bulletin, 22 (5)*:9-126, 1979.

Goodstein, L.D.: *Consulting with Human Service Systems*. Reading, Massachusetts, Addison-Wesley, 1978.

Halloran, J.: *Applied Human Relations: An Organizational Approach*. Englewood Cliffs, NJ, Prentice-Hall, 1978.

*Kadushin, A.: *Supervision in Social Work*. New York, Columbia University Press, 1976.

Lessinger, L.M.: Robbing Dr. Peter to "pay Paul": accounting for our stewardship in public education. *Educational Technology, 11*:11-20, 1971.

McGregor, D.: *The Human Side of Enterprise*. New York, McGraw-Hill, 1960.

Mitchell, C.M., Kantrowitz, R.E., and Davidson, W.S.: Differential attitude change in nonprofessional experience: An experimental comparison. *Journal of Counseling Psychology, 27*:625-629, 1980.

*Moses, H.A., and Hardin, J.T.: A relationship approach to counselor supervision in agency settings. In Boyd, J. (Ed.): *Counselor Supervision: Approaches, Preparation, Practices*. Muncie, IN, Accelerated Development, 1978, pp. 441-480.

Roark, A.E.: Interpersonal conflict management. *Personnel and Guidance Journal, 56*:400-402, 1978.

Schein, E.H.: *Process Consultation: Its Role in Organization Development*. Reading, Addison-Wesley, 1969.

Scriven, M.S.: The methodology of evaluation. In *Perspectives of Curriculum Evaluation*. American Educational Research Association Monograph, Series in Curriculum Evaluation, No. 11. Chicago, Rand McNally, 1967.

Tannenbaum, R., Weschler, I., and Massarik, F.: *Leadership and Organizations: A Behvaioral Science Approach*. New York, McGraw-Hill, 1961.

*White, S.L.: *Managing Health and Human Services Programs, A Guide for Managers*. New York, The Free Press, 1981.

---

*Recommended readings

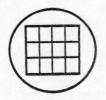

CHAPTER 9

GROUP APPROACHES
IN CONSULTATION AND SUPERVISION

CONSULTATION and supervision can be done both individually and in groups. As has been mentioned in the previous chapter, the two kinds of approaches are usually combined
since they effectively complement each other. This chapter offers
practical suggestions on applying group methodology to consultative and supervisory interventions. In terms of the Three-Dimensional Intervention Model, the chapter covers cells 2 — A, B, C, D
— I, II, III, as illustrated in Figure 9-1.

APPLICATION OF GROUP PRINCIPLES

Since most counseling practitioners are well acquainted with
group processes, a review of general principles of group work does
not seem necessary. However, it will be useful to examine to what
degree these principles apply to group consultation and supervision.

Group Definitions

Group counseling has been defined repeatedly and from various points of view (Mahler, 1969). One of the best-known definitions has been compiled by Gazda, Duncan, and Meadows (1967)
from forty-three responses to a survey of prominent group counselors. Whichever definition of group work one may prefer, it

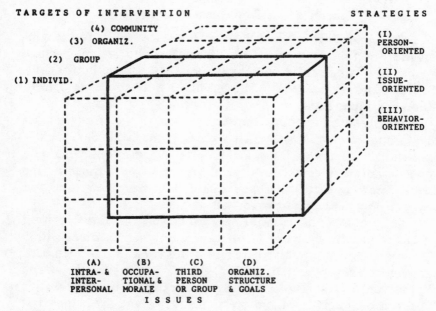

TARGETS OF INTERVENTION

(4) COMMUNITY
(3) ORGANIZ.
(2) GROUP
(1) INDIVID.

STRATEGIES

(I) PERSON-ORIENTED

(II) ISSUE-ORIENTED

(III) BEHAVIOR-ORIENTED

(A)
INTRA- &
INTER-
PERSONAL

(B)
OCCUPA-
TIONAL &
MORALE

(C)
THIRD
PERSON
OR GROUP

(D)
ORGANIZ.
STRUCTURE
& GOALS

ISSUES

Figure 9-1. Perimeter of Group Work in Consultation and Supervision (Solid Lines) within the Three-Dimensional Intervention Model (Dotted Lines).

always includes three basic elements that are common to group counseling, consultation, and supervision: (1) the physical presence of group members to each other, (2) common goals freely chosen by group members, and (3) a mutual interaction among group members.

By implication it is evident that consulting work done by correspondence or supervision based solely on individual contacts and written reports is not group work, no matter how many people are involved. Neither is it group work if consultees passively listen to the consultant without any interaction or exchange of ideas, as is typical of people in the audience at a formal address. Information presented in this chapter will demonstrate, however, that true group work is both possible and feasible in the field of consultation and supervision.

Efficiency and Effectiveness of Group Work

Efficiency of group work in human services refers to the conservation of time and effort by offering help to several persons at the same time rather than helping each person individually (Shertzer and Stone, 1976). This principle fully applies to consultation and supervision.

Effectiveness of group counseling refers to the strong impact that group interaction has on its participants, which frequently exceeds the effects of individual helping interventions. Sharing a concern or a problem with others is in itself reassuring for the client. Knowing that other people have similar problems makes it easier to cope with one's own distress.

The cohesive character of the group and the thrust toward goals common to all its members generate dynamic forces within the group that are highly therapeutic and enhance the members' problem-solving potential (Lifton, 1966; Dinkmeyer, Pew, and Dinkmeyer, 1979). Thus, the helping process in a group setting flows not only between the professional helper and the helpee, but also among the helpees themselves. This principle of group effectiveness in counseling fully applies to group consultation and supervision as well.

Group Rules and Group Climate

Authors (e.g. Mahler, 1969; Dinkmeyer and Muro, 1971; Gazda, 1976; Trotzer, 1977) generally agree that group members have to be aware of and committed to a set of ground rules, if the group process is to bring about positive outcomes. An example of a set of such ground rules follows:

1. Group members and group leaders are partners who are equally responsible for the success of the group process.
2. Group members have complete freedom to express their views and feelings.
3. To assure this freedom, group members are obligated to respect the personal dignity and rights of each other.
4. When disagreeing with their peers, group members must avoid offensive or demeaning verbal or nonverbal behavior.

5. Group members are to promote communication within the group and to lend support to others.

6. Group members have to observe the degree of confidentiality agreed upon by the group.

Ground rules used in counseling have to be modified for purposes of consultation and supervision according to specific circumstances.

The ground rules help establish a framework for the group process, protect the rights of individual members, and promote a nonthreatening, creative group climate. This is of major importance in group consultation and group supervision when participation by group members is required. The rules offer an assurance to group members that their individuality and personal freedom will be respected as long as they are willing to respect the rights of others.

Group Leadership Styles

Group leadership styles can be placed on a continuum similar to the one illustrated in Figure 8-2, from authoritarian to laissez faire. The styles vary according to the leader's personal traits, experiences, and values, and according to the purpose of the group (Dinkmeyer and Muro, 1971). However, it is usually wise to avoid either of the two extreme leadership approaches, total directiveness or no directiveness at all.

Another point that needs to be reemphasized is the difference between assigned authority and actual leadership. These two functions do not always coincide. Authority is generated outside of the group and is formally assigned to a person by management. The group may or may not be consulted before the assignment is made. By contrast, leadership is generated within the group and derived from acceptance of the leader by group members. Group leadership can never be imposed.

Consistent with the process orientation advocated in this book, participatory leadership seems most suited to group strategies in consultation and supervision, since it is based on partnership. Furthermore, the participatory leadership model is broad enough to accommodate a variety of operational patterns and personal styles.

Socio Groups and Psyche Groups

Jennings (1950) coined the concepts of *socio* and *psyche* groups and differentiated them as follows: Socio groups are primarily concerned with tangible products of the group interaction, whereas psyche groups are geared toward the emotional fulfillment of group members. Incidentally, this may remind us of a parallel distinction between person orientation and task orientation in supervisory processes, discussed in the previous chapter.

Coffey (1952) asserts that the socio and psyche group models are separate ends of the group process continuum rather than opposites in a true dichotomy. He considers their merger a necessary condition for optimal outcomes in group interventions and invokes the authority of Kurt Lewin to bolster his thesis: "Lewin saw the importance of incorporating into the socio group aspects of the problem-solving group the rich store of potential involvement, motivation, and ego fulfillment characteristic of the psyche group process. . . . And in every instance the goal of group productivity has led inevitably to finding ways and means of greater emotional investments of the individual in the socio-process of problem solving" (p. 52).*

The implication of Lewin's group dynamics movement for consultation and supervision can be summarized as follows: A balanced blending of psyche group concerns (people orientation) and of socio group concerns (task orientation) is likely to promote the most effective group interventions.

When to Use Group Approaches

As in counseling, group approaches to consultation and supervision are particularly appropriate in the following situations:

1. When consultants or supervisors want to generate or to improve communication and dialogue among consultees or supervisees
2. When they intend to get broad input on some issues and to arrive at a consensus of the group for problem resolution

---

*From Hubert S. Coffey, Socio and psyche group process: Integrative concepts. In C.G. Kemp, *Perspective on the Group Process*, 2nd ed., 1970. Originally published in *Journal of Social Issues*, Vol. 8, Spring 1952. Reprinted by permission.

3. When they wish to present information and obtain immediate feedback from the group

4. When they hope to involve a number of persons in learning new skills and practicing them with each other

Some issues involving extensive interaction within the group are better handled in small groups of five to ten persons (parallel to group counseling). Other processes that are informational in nature can be effectively accomplished in large groups (parallel to group guidance).

When Group Approaches Are Not Useful

Certain situations don't lend themselves to group work, and individual consultation or supervision may be preferable. Myrick (n.d.) lists the following instances:

1. When confidentiality is essential for successful outcomes of the intervention

2. When the helper confronts a crisis that requires immediate action

3. When the helpee feels threatened by a group setting

4. When the helper foresees that personal counseling may be needed as part of the intervention

5. When there are circumstances that prevent the formation of group cohesiveness

It is beyond the scope of this book to delve any deeper into group theory or the training of group leaders. Readers who wish to review specific issues in group work are referred to the titles listed at the end of this chapter.

GROUP CONSULTATION WITH TEACHERS

When serving as group consultants, counselors frequently work with teachers. There are still many ambivalent feelings among teachers toward group work, which may account for its underuse, particularly in secondary school settings. Masson and Jacobs (1980) have found that even some counselors do not feel comfortable with group work, either because they do not possess adequate leadership skills or because they have experienced failure in the past. Some teachers may have formed negative attitudes while exposed to poorly run groups or to unethical group practices, e.g. to encounter experiences in which abusive behavior was tolerated by the group leader, as reported by Gazda, Duncan, and Sisson (1971). No matter what the causes may be, avoiding group work handicaps both counselors and teachers, since their professional success depends on group-related skills.

This realization underscores the need for group experiences in consultation that prove to be valuable in the professional domain and are personally satisfying to consultees. By its nature, group methodology is a powerful, two-pronged instrument; it helps people (1) solve their personal or occupational problems and (2) improve their social skills through the group process. In other words, the process and the outcomes merge and are dynamically integrated. A parallel phenomenon of such a dynamic merger in the field of communication has been pointed out by Marshall McLuhan in his well-known axiom, "the medium is the message" (McLuhan and Fiore, 1967). When applied to group work, the *medium* stands for the group process and the *message* stands for the outcomes. The group process can be used in virtually all consultation work, particularly with teachers and parents:

1. In client-centered consultation, in which the focus is on solving the problems of students
2. In consultee-centered consultation, which concentrates on professional educators or parents, by teaching educational skills or by providing emotional support
3. In institutional consultation, which focuses on organizational development

Concerns and Needs of Teachers

Teachers are generally receptive to consultation projects that focus on their true professional concerns and meet their personal needs. For this reason, it is useful to conduct a preliminary survey of faculty preferences as to issues to be dealt with in the consultation project. Other topics suggested by administrators or students should be added to the list, which then provides a realistic basis for selecting a central issue. It is important to prepare at least a rudimentary topical agenda and to keep it flexible enough for adjustments to the actual needs of the group consultees. What follows is a list of current teacher concerns selected from various sources, including teacher training centers:

1. To understand students as individuals and to respond to their instructional needs
2. To improve the classroom atmosphere and to promote self-discipline among students (Tanaka, 1979)
3. To use mainstreaming effectively and to be sensitive to the unique needs of exceptional and culturally different students (Brown, Wyne, Blackburn, and Powell, 1979)
4. To promote students' motivation for self-improvement
5. To help students develop career-awareness (Sklare, 1977)
6. To effectively relate to parents of students, particularly of handicapped students (Burggraf, 1979)
7. To help improve cooperation among professional personnel of the school (Knoblock and Goldstein, 1971)
8. To counteract the burnout syndrome among faculty (Edelwich and Brodsky, 1980)

This list may serve as a point of departure for initiating teacher groups when no pressing needs can be identified. However, the topical area has to be identified and narrowed down either (1) before the group consultation project begins so that teachers know what they may expect or (2) at the first group meeting, if the teachers opt for an open agenda.

Types of Teacher Groups

Washburn (1978) makes a distinction between student-centered group consultation and teacher support groups, which closely approximate group counseling. (It should be added that student-centered consultation often blends with teacher-centered instructional processes.) In terms of the topics in the preceding list, items 1-6 fall in the category of student-centered consultation; items 7 and 8 fall in the category of teacher support groups.

To facilitate interaction and to promote cohesiveness of the group, the seating arrangements for participants in any group should be in a circle rather than theater style. All three helping strategies discussed in Chapter 5 — person-oriented, issue-oriented, and behavior-oriented strategies — may be used. However, in student-centered or consultee-centered group work, task orientation is prevalent, with a strong emphasis on problem solving and skills acquisition. By contrast, support groups are predominately person-oriented, focusing on the teachers' subjective world and on their personal and social needs. Yet, skillful group leaders are able to maintain a basic linkage of the two orientations in any group format, which explains why enhanced ego strength of the participants is frequently the side effect of task-oriented groups.

Gordon's T.E.T. Program

Several models of teacher consultation groups have been proposed during the last fifteen years. Gordon (1974) has developed the widely used Teacher Effectiveness Training (T.E.T.) program, which consists of weekly three-hour training sessions typically spread over a ten-week period. The approach emphasizes communication skills, such as "active" listening by which the teacher enters the world of the student and attempts to perceive reality from his or her vantage point (*cf.* the phenomenological approach, p. 60). This encourages increased communication between students and teachers and among students themselves. Decision making within the class is participatory with appropriate student involvement. When problems arise, the teacher resolves them with the help of the class rather than attempting to do so alone.

The Adlerian Approach

Another approach to teacher training was proposed by Adlerian psychologists and has found many adherents during the past decade. This teacher training model grew out of the efforts by Rudolf Dreikurs, whose aim was the establishment of child guidance centers with Adlerian methodology (Dreikurs, 1948; Dreikurs and Soltz, 1964; Dinkmeyer, Pew, and Dinkmeyer, 1979). Emphasis is placed on the goal orientation of individual behavior and on the need for promoting self-directiveness, responsibility, and social consciousness. Most problems originate through faulty social interaction, and they can be corrected by helping individuals engage in healthy group interaction. For instance, class members should be encouraged to cooperate with each other rather than to compete. An effective teacher should be aware of the four mistaken goals of youth misbehavior — attention getting, power, revenge, and display of inadequacy — and counteract such misbehavior by corrective strategies (Dinkmeyer and Carlson, 1973).

Specific Adlerian Programs

Some Adlerian group leaders prefer a structured study plan, and they use various resource materials, such as the S.T.E.T. kit (which includes a manual, *Systematic Training for Effective Teaching,* and other resources, e.g. instructional tapes) developed by Dinkmeyer, McKay, and Dinkmeyer (1980) or the book of Dreikurs and Cassel (1972), *Discipline without Tears,* in tandem with Gwen Drapela's (1977) *Leader's Guide for Teacher Study Groups.* The S.T.E.T. sequence consists of fourteen meetings, each two to three hours long. The latter program is shorter, consisting of eight to ten weekly meetings, each lasting about one hour.

Others may draw the agenda for discussions, problem solving, and learning experiences from the group itself. An interesting model of this kind, which has been proposed by Dinkmeyer (1971), is known as *C-Groups.* The *C* in the title stands for collaboration, consultation, communication, concern and caring, confidentiality, and commitment. These focal elements give a clear indication of the nature of C-Groups, which are limited in size (four to six teachers) and meet once a week for one hour, six to eight times.

The small size facilitates personal involvement of group participants who are encouraged to present work-related problems that are solved on the basis of Adlerian principles. The didactic material provided for the group is limited to handouts dealing with the nature of C-Groups, the basic Adlerian approach, and ways of identifying the goals of children's misbehavior.

Parenthetically, it can be added that group leaders who prefer an open-agenda approach in teacher consultation will find a useful framework for the group process in the stages of consultation discussed in Chapter 4. For example a problem-solving group, drawing its agenda from members, would likely include the following stages: establishing group rapport, exploring central issues or problems, setting goals, reviewing available options, making and implementing decisions, and evaluating outcomes.

PARENT GROUP CONSULTATION

Almost all that has been said about teacher group consultation also applies to group consultation with parents. Dinkmeyer and Carlson (1973) list among the basic objectives of parent group consultation the following:

1. To help parents understand and improve their relationship with children
2. To help parents improve their communication with children
3. To help parents understand the importance of the family for children
4. To promote coordination of efforts exerted by the school and the home for a balanced upbringing of children

Models of Parent Consultation

The most popular parent groups currently in use closely approximate the models of teacher consultation. Most parent groups chronologically preceded the teacher consultation programs (Schlossman, 1976). One major innovation is the single-parent group consultation model (Green, 1981). The emphasis on single-parent consultation will undoubtedly increase in view of the prediction that nearly 50 percent of all children presently being born will live in single-parent households before reaching adulthood.

Gordon's P.E.T. Program

Gordon's (1970) Parent Effectiveness Training (P.E.T.) has been in existence for over a decade. The program focuses on improving the parents' communication skills, on balancing the needs of parents and children, and on preventing parent-child conflicts before they emerge. Gordon advocates parent-child relationships in which both parent and child feel comfortable and conflict resolutions in which both the parent and the child are winners. The P.E.T. program consists of twenty-four hours of lectures and practical learning through demonstrations, tape recordings, role playing, and group discussions.

Adlerian Programs

As mentioned earlier, Dreikurs (1948) pioneered Adlerian family and parent consultation as long as three decades ago. The emphasis was on the role of the family as the basic social group and the predominant influence in the child's life. This is also the underlying rationale of Dinkmeyer and McKay's (1976) program of Systematic Training for Effective Parenting (S.T.E.P.).

S.T.E.P. is a nine-week study program structured in a group format. The group leader has the use of a resource kit containing a leader's manual, parent handbooks, group discussion charts, instructional tapes, and other materials. The S.T.E.P. format can be applied in various configurations of activities and adjusted to varied degrees of structure to meet the needs of the parent group. Participants are helped to understand the difference between effective and ineffective behaviors in dealing with their children. The leader provides theoretical insights, initiates learning experiences, and helps the parents set realistic goals for their efforts. Members are encouraged to share their experiences with the group and to help each other overcome obstacles.

Another Adlerian approach to parent education is Dinkmeyer's C-Group format for teachers adapted to the needs of parents. The goals and methods of both kinds of C-Groups are similar (Dinkmeyer, Pew, and Dinkmeyer, 1979).

Goodyear and Rubovits (1982) propose a parent education program that combines the Adlerian approach with Gordon's (1970) P.E.T. emphasis on communication within the family. They use Maslow's hierarchy of needs as a framework for organizing components of the program, starting with family survival through behavior management and moving up to the highest levels (esteem, self-actualization, etc.) through improved communication. This model is particularly recommended for low income, single parents who operate at the level of physiological needs.

Other Models

Several other models of family group consultation have been developed in the past two decades. However, because of their structure and methodological approach, many of them belong in the category of family counseling or family therapy rather than family consultation. Their common strategy is the treatment of the entire family as a group within its own dynamic setting (McComb, 1981).

An example of this approach is Fullmer's (1976) family group consultation model. The family treatment group includes not only parents and children, but also grandparents, uncles and aunts, and friends of the family. In cases of families with only parents and children, two or three families are combined within the therapy group. Fullmer (1976) envisions four distinct goals for the family group consultation, which he ranks from least to most demanding in terms of effort required: "Interpersonal skill development; conflict resolution within the family; major redefinition of relationship within the family; massive redefinition of relationship within the family and the public" (p. 286). Depending on the nature of the goal to be achieved, the length of the family group work will range from one or two sessions to several months or years.

GROUP APPROACHES TO COUNSELOR SUPERVISION

Group supervision is used both with counselors in training and with counseling practitioners. The principal reasons for using groups are —

1. To promote cooperation, cohesiveness, and mutual support among staff members or counselors in training
2. To facilitate an ongoing exchange of professional experiences and group consultation, especially in complex counseling cases
3. To provide a forum for regular discussions of organizational issues that require group input, such as agency or department policies

Staff Meetings

Although the climate of all staff meetings should be informal and the interaction of staff members spontaneous, the supervisor needs to provide a basic structure by preparing an agenda, preferably to be circulated among members ahead of the meeting. A supervisor who balances task orientation with people orientation will help the group adhere to the agenda without stifling occasional digressions that may involve personal concerns or spontaneous comments on other areas of staff functioning. A staff meeting that flounders or one in which no substantive issues are discussed is a waste of time and a discourtesy to professional colleagues.

It is useful to have occasional open-agenda meetings or brainstorming sessions. Havelock (1973) emphasizes that such meetings must be announced in advance to allow participants to prepare for them. At all meetings, someone should be responsible for taking notes and prepare minutes, which should later be distributed to all staff members for further reference (White, 1981). This helps prevent disputes and misunderstandings in the future.

Practicum or Internship Seminars

Practicum or internship seminars are scheduled once a week during the entire field experience of counselors in training, and each meeting usually lasts from two to three hours. All general recommendations made for the group process apply here, e.g. leadership style, ground rules, and seating arrangement in the room. The group emphasis is on learning through sharing and on discussion of experiences in the field. Students also listen to each other's tapes and provide an analysis and critique of their interview processes and dynamics. The group experience helps students realize that they are not alone in facing certain problems. The understanding and support of the group help individuals gain self-confidence and professional maturity.

SUMMARY

1. The general principles of group work also apply to group approaches in consultation and supervision. Among these princi-

ples are the basic elements of the group definition, the principle of group efficiency and effectiveness, the requirement of ground rules for group work, the continuum of leadership styles, and the theoretical distinction between socio and psyche groups.

2. Group approaches are particularly appropriate in those consultation or supervision projects that require interaction of all involved persons or call for immediate feedback. Group approaches are not recommended in situations where the group would endanger confidentiality, be threatening, or be otherwise ineffective.

3. Group consultation with teachers needs to be geared to their current professional concerns and personal needs, which should be identified by a survey.

4. Examples of widely used teacher groups are listed; they include Gordon's Teacher Effectiveness Training and several Adlerian approaches.

5. Parent group consultation programs are similar to teacher groups, both in content and methodology. Examples of currently used parent consultation programs are reviewed along with family counseling work, which is occasionally called family consultation.

6. Group approaches are equally important in educational supervision of counselors in training and in administrative supervision of counseling practitioners.

REFERENCES

Brown, D., Wyne, M.D., Blackburn, J.E., and Powell, W.C.: *Consultation: Strategy for Improving Education.* Boston, Allyn and Bacon, 1979.

Burgraff, M.Z.: Consulting with parents of handicapped children. *Elementary School Guidance and Counseling, 13*:215-221, 1979.

Coffey, H.S.: Socio and psyche group process: Integrative concepts. In Kemp, C.G.: *Perspective on the Group Process,* 2nd ed. Boston, Houghton Mifflin, 1970, pp. 47-55.

Dinkmeyer, D., and Carlson, J.: *Consulting: Facilitating Human Potential and Change Processes.* Columbus, OH, Merrill, 1973.

Dinkmeyer, D., and McKay, G.: *Systematic Training for Effective Parenting.* Circle Pines, MN, American Guidance Service, 1976.

*Dinkmeyer, D., McKay, G., and Dinkmeyer, D., Jr.: *S.T.E.T. Kit.* Circle Pines, MN, American Guidance Service, 1980.

*Recommended reading

*Dinkmeyer, D., and Muro, J.J.: *Group Counseling: Theory and Practice.* Itasca, IL, Peacock, 1971.

Dinkmeyer, D., Pew, W.L., and Dinkmeyer, D.C., Jr.: *Adlerian Counseling and Psychotherapy.* Monterey, CA, Brooks/Cole, 1979.

Drapela, G.B.: *Leader's Guide for Teacher Study Groups.* Chicago, Alfred Adler Institute, 1977.

Dreikurs, R., and Soltz, V.: *Children: The Challenge.* New York, Hawthorne, 1964.

Edelwich, J., and Brodsky, A.: *Burn-out: Stages of Disillusionment in the Helping Professions.* New York, Human Services Press, 1980.

Fullmer, D.W.: Family group consultation. In Gazda, G.M. (Ed.): *Theories and Methods of Group Counseling in the Schools.* Springfield, IL, Thomas, 1976, pp. 285-312.

*Gazda, G.M. (Ed.): *Theories and Methods of Group Counseling in the Schools.* Springfield, IL, Thomas, 1976.

Gazda, G.M., Duncan, J.A., and Meadows, M.E.: Group counseling and group procedures — report of a survey. *Counselor Education and Supervision, 6*:306-310, 1967.

Gazda, G.M., Duncan, J.A., and Sisson, P.J.: Professional issues in group work. *Personnel and Guidance Journal, 49*:637-643, 1971.

Goodyear, R.K., and Rubovits, J.J.: Parent education: A model for low-income parents. *Personnel and Guidance Journal, 60*:409-412, 1982.

*Gordon, T.: *Parent Effectiveness Training.* New York, Peter H. Wyden, 1970.

Green, B.J.: Helping single-parent families. *Elementary School Guidance and Counseling, 15*:249-261, 1981.

Havelock, R.G.: *The Change Agent's Guide to Innovation in Education.* Englewood Cliffs, NJ, Educational Technology Publications, 1973.

Jennings, H.H.: *Leadership and Isolation,* 2nd ed. New York, Longmans-Green, 1950.

Knoblock, P., and Goldstein, A.P.: *The Lonely Teacher.* Boston, Allyn and Bacon, 1971.

Lifton, W.M.: *Working with Groups: Group Process and Individual Growth,* 2nd ed. New York, Wiley, 1966.

Mahler, C.A.: *Group Counseling in the Schools.* Boston, Houghton Mifflin, 1969.

Masson, R.L., and Jacobs, E.: Group leadership: Practical points for beginners. *Personnel and Guidance Journal, 59*:52-55, 1980.

McComb, B. (Ed.): Family counseling (special issue). *Elementary School Guidance and Counseling, 15*:180-279, 1981.

McLuhan, H.M., and Fiore, Q.: *The Medium is the Message.* New York, Random House, 1967.

---

*Recommended readings

*Myrick, R.D.: *Consultation as a Counselor Intervention.* Ann Arbor, MI, ERIC/CAPS, not dated.

Schlossman, S.L.: Before home start: Notes toward a history of parent education in America, 1897-1929. *Harvard Educational Review, 46*:436-467, 1976.

Shertzer, B., and Stone, S.C.: *Fundamentals of Guidance,* 3rd ed. Boston, Houghton Mifflin, 1976.

Sklare, A.: Career consulting: Utilizing the Delphi technique with career education content. *Elementary School Guidance and Counseling, 11*: 309-315, 1977.

Tanaka, J.: *Classroom Management, A Guide for the School Consultant.* Springfield, Thomas, 1979.

*Trotzer, J.P.: *The Counselor and the Group: Integrating Theory, Training, and Practice.* Monterey, CA, Brooks/Cole, 1977.

*Washburn, H.R.: Getting started with teacher groups. *Elementary School Guidance and Counseling, 13*:56-64, 1978.

White, S.L.: *Managing Health and Human Services Programs: A Guide for Managers.* New York, Free Press, 1981.

---

*Recommended readings

Section III
PROMOTING CHANGE IN INSTITUTIONS AND THE COMMUNITY

THIS section of the book deals with counselor interventions for promoting changes and improvements in organizational and community environments. The concept of change agentry is based on the premise that clients cannot be adequately helped unless pathogenic influences in their environment are removed or at least diminished. Chapter 10 reviews the historical roots, the nature, and the operational patterns of change agentry and emphasizes the close relationship of change agentry and consultation.

Chapter 11 applies the process of change agentry to institutional settings and industrial organizations. It focuses on diagnosing healthy and unhealthy organizational patterns and applying the methodology of organization development (OD) to work with educational and human services institutions.

Chapter 12 explores the opportunities for outreach programs in the community. The concept of the community and community dynamics are explored, and operational patterns for dealing with community issues are proposed. Particular consideration is given to identifying community problems that need attention and to effectively using community resources and political processes for support of outreach programs. The chapter concludes with a brief explanation of evaluation procedures for change agentry projects both in institutions and in the community at large.

CHAPTER 10

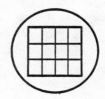

COUNSELORS AS CHANGE AGENTS
HISTORICAL ROOTS OF CHANGE AGENTRY

ALTHOUGH current trends toward social activism and change agentry seem relatively recent phenomena, their origins can be traced back to the early years of this century. At that time, several psychologists, particularly Alfred Adler, Erich Fromm, and Karen Horney, began questioning the prevalent Freudian view that inborn instincts were the principal determinants of human behavior. Instead, they emphasized the major role of social and cultural influences in shaping a person's development and affecting the level of mental health. Philosophically committed to social humanism, they were concerned about the many pathogenic forces within modern society and deplored the unauthentic, depersonalized way of modern life.

In his analysis of social structures in the Western world, Fromm (1955) presented a scathing criticism of the dehumanizing impact that the twentieth century's cult of industry and commerce exerted on the average person. Both he and Adler (1964) advocated far-reaching institutional changes that would lead to a society rooted in brotherliness and solidarity and would mold mankind into a cooperating community. Between World Wars I and II, these idealistic principles had a major impact on some social psychologists, who attempted to translate them into operational patterns. Kurt Lewin (1951) is being singled out as one of the most influential protagonists of institutional change to be attained primarily through group dynamics. In his view, striking a balance between the needs of individuals and institutions was an important step toward social reform.

In more recent years, the idea of change agentry has sprung up in education and other human services. For instance, Benne and Muntyan (1951) pioneered change agentry in schools and promoted positive interpersonal relationships through curricular renewal. Bennis, Benne, and Chin (1969) advocated change in all areas of social services, and Havelock (1973) developed a systematic approach to innovation processes in the field of education.

Counselors got involved in institutional change during the intense social activism of the 1960s. One of the first indications of counselor dissatisfaction with the status quo was the call for altering the scope of counselor functioning (1) beyond the therapeutic domain, (2) away from administrative tasks, and (3) toward student advocacy (Lortie, 1965). This initial trend toward social involvement was applied in subsequent years to the area of institutional structures, particularly in the school system. Cook (1972) defined institutional change agentry as a natural extension of the work of school counselors. Recently, Walz and Benjamin (1977, 1978) have summarized the current thinking on change agentry processes and strategies.

Change agentry is undoubtedly an exciting new professional challenge. Change is the dynamic force that maintains the vitality of any society, institution, or profession. Throughout history, all social progress has been the result of change. However, history also proves that not all changes have led to improvements; some have resulted in significant setbacks. This insight may be an important caveat for those of us who wish to have a positive and lasting impact on society. Change agentry is too important a tool to be used unwisely or irresponsibly.

CHANGE AGENTRY AND THE COUNSELING PROFESSION

Traditionally, counselors have focused their efforts on individual or group counseling, but they often saw little therapeutic change in clients who remained in unhealthy environmental settings. As Walz and Benjamin (1977) point out, counselors have come to realize that many behavioral problems are not self-generated by clients but are caused "by sick systems, organizations or groups that impact negatively upon the people within them. So-called maladaptive behavior or client problems may in reality be client strengths — clients are unwilling to accept what the system is asking of them, and with justification" (pp. 3-4). It was precisely this realization that has moved counselors toward change agentry. Many of them have felt that adjusting their role from an exclusively therapeutic model to a strategy that combined direct help (counseling) with indirect help (promoting institutional change) was in the best interest of their clients.

Radical Positions

When new social phenomena emerge, they often move through a radical stage before reaching their final, productive form. This was also the case with change agentry by counselors. Certain promoters of the new trend assumed radical positions and advocated extreme solutions. Rather than pressing for changes in institutions, they called for the abolishment of present social structures, which they considered beyond help. Furthermore, traditional counseling and social activism were portrayed as mutually exclusive. It was suggested that counselors who wish to become change agents should abandon their basic professional functions. For instance, Adams (1974) advocated the cessation of vocational guidance since it facilitated the exploitation of individuals and large scale achievement and intelligence testing since it stratified the population. He also opposed crisis intervention and personal adjustment counseling. In his view, the former merely kept a lid on explosive situations, particularly in schools, and the latter tended to convince clients that the source of alienation was within themselves. Counselors were urged to help clients band together and combat the existing social structure in favor of a new society "based on cooperation, equality and collectivism" (Adams, 1974, p. 537).

Such radical attitudes have generally proven counterproductive for advancing change agentry. Furthermore, they have hurt the public image of the counseling profession, raised questions about the counselors' professional commitments, and reinforced the clamor for accountability in counseling and guidance programs.

The Affirmative View of Change Agentry

By now, extremist positions have largely lost their appeal, and an affirmative and realistic frame of reference has prevailed. Change agents are well aware of the ills of society and of the dehumanizing influences that some existing social structures exert upon people. However, they realize that a negativist approach will not eliminate the current ills. They see the aims of their efforts in terms of renewal of institutions through process consultation (Schein, 1969) and through organizational development approaches (Burke and Goodstein, 1980).

Havelock (1973) has accurately expressed the positive orientation of this new breed of change agents, one characterized by vigor and optimism. The aim of affirmative innovations and changes is a "significant alteration in the status quo . . . which is intended to benefit the people involved" (p. 4). Affirmative change agentry avoids polarizing people into adversary groups and promotes instead solutions that benefit everybody. In spite of institutional resistance to change (Blake and Mouton, 1976), affirmative change agents, some of them counselors, have brought about significant institutional reforms in recent years.

THE NATURE OF CHANGE AGENTRY

Change agentry is not a temporary involvement — an isolated action or a series of interventions — no matter how impressive. Rather, it is a personal commitment, a philosophical orientation based on the belief that every individual has an inner worth, that society's health depends on the well-being of individuals, and that institutions are meant to serve people rather than themselves. Change agentry parallels human rights advocacy; it promotes people's legitimate interests within institutions (the family, the school, the employing organization, and the community at large) and helps establish or reestablish a healthy balance between task-oriented and person-oriented concerns in organizational systems.

Although institutional innovations are the ultimate goals of change agentry, they cannot be achieved without gradual changes in people's attitudes. It is people who control organizational structures, establish institutional policies, and set corporate goals.

Promoting changes in organizational structures means promoting changes in people, particularly in people who have influence and make decisions. (In this context, any helping intervention, such as individual and group counseling, is a tool of change agentry.) Changing people's attitudes, of course, takes time and requires tact and patience paired with clear goal orientation and persistence on the part of the change agent. However, when enough people become sensitive to a problem they ignored in the past, and especially when they are willing to "assume ownership" of the problem, institutional innovations occur relatively fast.

The paramount skill of a change agent consists of the ability to speak loudly enough to make people aware of and interested in the problem and eventually to help them adopt the problem as their own (Walz and Benjamin, 1977), but not so loudly as to take center stage and thus detract attention from the problem. Change agentry is not meant to be an ego trip. Many highly successful innovations have come about through efforts of people whose names are virtually unknown.

Who Can Be Change Agents

Change agentry is the responsibility of every concerned person in an institution. However, the counselor and the administrator are particularly suited for the task, although they approach it from opposite directions (Paul, 1982). Either of the two roles has its own advantages. Administrators who work from above have more clout to provide resources and to organizationally involve others in the project. Conversely, counselors working from below have the advantage of being equals to their co-workers. They can stimulate more spontaneous cooperation, form closer bonds of commitment with fellow change agents, and have firsthand knowledge of group dynamics among staff members and clients of the agency or students of the school.

The question arises whether or not paid consultants can serve as concerned, humanistic agents of change. There is no doubt that they can. It depends, of course, on the consultant's personal philosophy and ethical integrity as to how he or she will handle the consultation project. Consultants who are highly professional in their attitudes will have the courage to withstand and counteract pressures exerted on them by an insensitive managerial staff and will not overlook dehumanizing conditions that exist in the organizational system. They will feel duty-bound to press for a healthy balance between task orientation and people orientation in order to improve worker morale and to increase productivity.

Paid consultants may not argue the issues from a strictly humanistic point of view, but they will point out to management that ignoring the legitimate needs of employees and failing to involve workers as active participants in the organization's development is contrary to the pragmatic interests of the system. This argumentation may be more convincing than philosophical reasoning when consultants deal with highly cost-conscious administrators. It should be added that many professional consultants working for a fee have proven their genuine humanistic concerns; they have often enhanced their clout with management by their reputation reflected in the fees they charged.

OPERATIONAL PATTERNS OF CHANGE AGENTRY

From the preceding discussion it should be clear that change agentry is not a set of techniques or strategies, but a philosophical orientation that is translated into operational patterns. Among the helping interventions discussed thus far in this volume the following can be used for change agentry:

1. Individual consultation with professionals and nonprofessionals
2. Group consultation with counselors, teachers, and parents
3. Educational and administrative supervision

However, the most effective instruments for changing the environment are —

4. Institutional consultation
5. Community outreach programs

These two topics will be discussed in Chapters 11 and 12.

Processes and Stages of Change Agentry

Since consultation is the strategy best suited for innovation projects, the processes and stages of consultation that were discussed in Chapter 4 are equally applicable to change agentry. When we speak of the process dimension, we mean more than a planned progress through a series of continuous actions toward a goal; we also imply that the aim of the helping intervention is an ongoing process of renewal rather than a neatly packaged product. What the change agent has done for a group of people during the helping intervention, the group is to continue doing for itself after the change agent has faded away.

Gordon Lippitt (1973), Havelock (1973), and Walz and Benjamin (1977) are among the authors who have addressed the issue of operational steps or stages in innovation processes. For reasons of clarity and consistency, the practical recommendations made here for the benefit of counselors — change agents — are arranged according to the consultation stages discussed in Chapter 4. Before reading on, it may be useful to review the sequence of consultation stages. What follows is an application of those stages to change agentry, particularly for counselors who wish to become change agents within their own organizations.

First Stage: Decision to Assume the Role of a Change Agent

Before getting involved in an innovative project, the counselor has to become fully committed to the cause of change agentry and be willing to invest sufficient time and energy in the project without neglecting the legitimate needs of clients. Although the field of innovation is never free of risks, the novice change agent should be careful to minimize them. It is a wise decision to start with small projects and succeed. This paves the road for success in more ambitious projects at a later date.

Second Stage: Entry, Rapport Building, Agreement on Team Work

The change agent needs to contact like-minded persons in the organization and ask for their cooperation. Walz and Benjamin (1977) recommend involving both formal authority figures (at least indirectly) and informal leaders, representatives of interest groups, and "gatekeepers," i.e. people who affect the flow of information within the organization. The initial personal contacts set the stage for a group meeting. The change agent assumes the role of group leader, briefly reviews the factors that led to the innovation project (e.g. burnout symptoms among teachers, complaints about lack of cooperation of staff members, etc.) and solicits input of group members. Once the group assumes ownership of the problem, it will handle the innovation project as a team intervention (Wigtil and Kelsey, 1978). This is a major success in itself, particularly if team members assume concrete responsibilities for promoting the project. An example of a successful collaborative approach to internal innovation of secondary guidance services within a school district is offered by Carrington, Cleveland, and Ketterman (1978).

Third Stage: Exploration and Diagnosis of the Problem

In addition to what has been suggested in the third stage of consultation, the change agent who has succeeded in forming a collaborative team should involve all team members in the exploration of the problem. This will lead toward group consensus on the diagnosis. At this point, Havelock (1973) suggests the use of a diagnostic inventory that assesses the following:

1. Goals of the system
2. Structure for achieving such goals
3. Degree of open communication
4. Resources of the system for achieving its goals
5. Rewards for members of the system who work toward achieving the goals

Another helpful diagnostic strategy recommended by Lippitt and Lippitt (1978) is the force-field analysis, based on Kurt Lewin's field theory. It lends itself well to group input, particularly to brainstorming by group members. All forces promoting improvement and change (persons, groups, material resources, etc.) and all forces opposing improvement and change (persons, groups, financial restrictions, procedures, environmental factors, etc.) are drawn in a diagram on a chalkboard or on a newsprint sheet. Each force is symbolized by a vector, its arrow indicating the direction of the force and its length indicating the strength of the force. An example of a force-field analysis assessing the relative strength of forces promoting and opposing improvement in a school is shown in Figure 10-1.

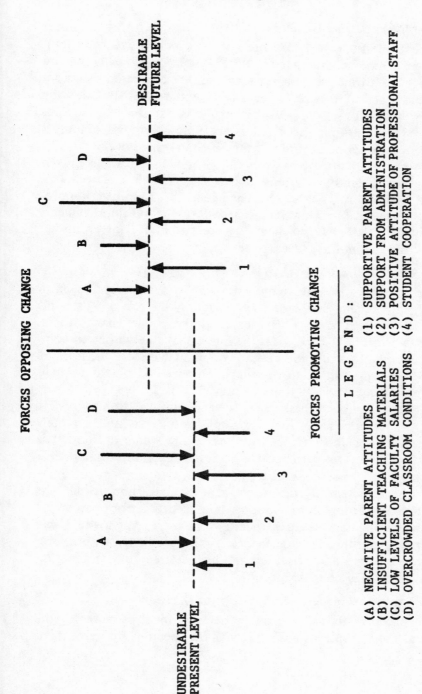

Figure 10-1. Force-Field Analysis in a School. On the left is the present level of performance, and on the right is the desirable future level.

Fourth Stage: Setting Goals

The force-field analysis approach not only helps the group arrive at a more comprehensive diagnosis, but also spells out the current state of affairs (where we now are) as compared to a more desirable state of affairs (where we intend to be). It helps the change agent set realistic goals by providing data on the resources and the restraints on the way toward innovation and pinpoints areas in which action should be taken if change is to occur.

It should be added that even a modest change that has proven its usefulness tends to stimulate additional changes later. This should be kept in mind while setting goals for the innovation project. Rather than striving for immediate and total improvement, the change agent may consider the current project as an initial, substantial step in the process of renewal.

Fifth Stage: Exploring Options

For creating a wide range of options, Walz and Benjamin (1977) recommend brainstorming, guided by the following ground rules: "Any idea goes. Each person deserves the chance to be heard. No criticism of an idea is allowed. If one wishes to comment on the ideas of another, the comment will take the form of piggy-backing — adding to or offering a variation on the original speaker's theme. Positive thinking prevails" (p. 27).

Group members may need advance information on what other institutions have done in similar situations and on their experiences — which approaches worked and which did not. It is helpful for the group to receive personal reactions from people who have had experience in using a particular program or to observe the program in operation at the institution which has adopted it. To explore options intelligently, group members also need to review data gathered during the diagnostic stage. Depending on the focal elements of the problem (people, procedures, resource allocation, etc.), which strategy or combination of strategies may be most useful?

Sixth Stage: Making and Implementing a Decision

In practical terms, to make a decision involves matching the most attractive options available with the specific requirements of the concrete situation. An ideal match may not be possible, but the group certainly will find a match that is both desirable and attainable. The decision must always contain an operational plan for implementation – who does what and how. At this crucial point, the group leader must press for a speedy implementation of the operational plan lest the momentum of the project is lost.

Seventh Stage: Evaluation of Final Outcomes

The group that has implemented the change should meet periodically to evaluate the outcomes as they emerge. No change is final; there is always room for additional improvement. However, if the change proves to be obviously impractical or counterproductive, the group has to recycle the process and come up with an acceptable alternative. Change agents should always practice the principle of fluid ideation. By being dogmatic or inflexible, change agents compromise their own credibility.

Eighth Stage: Termination of the Project

As has been stated earlier, the last stage of consultation requires a gradual, nonthreatening disengagement of the consultant from the helping relationship. This requirement also applies to change agentry. In every successful innovative project, a point is reached at which the counselor should step back and let a group of other committed people take full responsibility for the future course of the initiated process of change.

ENRICHMENT OF THE COUNSELOR'S PROFESSIONAL LIFE

It is in the nature of the change agentry that it generates new motivational forces. The counselor, who has tackled one innovative project, will soon discover that another intervention is needed. Change agentry adds a new dimension to the counselor's professional life, as it constantly challenges his or her awareness and creativity. Being aware of a problem situation leads to assuming ownership of it, which in turn requires an intervention towards change. And the cycle repeats itself.

Counselors who are change agents refuse to stand still in a world that is in flux. Individuals, groups, institutions, and society itself are in constant need of change and renewal. What had been considered an exciting innovation about five years ago may have since become an obsolescent phenomenon that needs updating, expanding, or refining. By its nature, change agentry is ageless and universal, and its challenges are never-ending.

SUMMARY

1. Change agentry has its roots in the efforts of humanistic social psychologists, e.g. Adler and Fromm, who advocated social changes for the benefit of individuals and mankind.

2. Among counselors, change agentry emerged as a new trend about twenty years ago, at first in the form of student advocacy and later focusing upon institutions themselves. Its interpretation has gone through a radical stage prior to assuming its present affirmative format.

3. Change agentry is a personal commitment based on solid convictions rather than merely a series of activities. Any helping intervention can be used in the process of change agentry.

4. Although every concerned person can become a change agent, supervisors and counselors are in a particularly favorable position to promote institutional change.

5. The process and stages of change agentry have been discussed with special reference to involvement of counselors within their own institutions.

6. Because of its ongoing challenges, change agentry conveys a new dimension to the professional life of counselors.

REFERENCES

Adams, H.J.: The progressive heritage of guidance: A view from the left. *Personnel and Guidance Journal, 51*:531-538, 1973.

Adler, A.: *Superiority and Social Interest: A Collection of Later Writings.* Evanston, IL, Northwestern University Press, 1964.

Benne, K.D., and Muntyan, B, (Eds.): *Human Relations in Curriculum Change.* New York, Dryden, 1951.

Bennis, W.G., Benne, K.D., and Chin, R. (Eds.): *The Planning of Change,* 2nd ed. New York, Holt, Rinehart and Winston, 1969.

Blake, R.R., and Mouton, J.S.: *Consultation.* Reading, MA, Addison-Wesley, 1976.

Burke, W.W., and Goodstein, L.D.: *Trends and Issues in OD: Current Theory and Practice.* San Diego, University Associates, 1980.

*Carrington, D., Cleveland, A., and Ketterman, C.: Collaborative consultation in the secondary schools. *Personnel and Guidance Journal, 56*:355-358, 1978.

Cook, D.R.: The change agent counselor — a conceptual context. *The School Counselor, 20*:9-15, 1972.

Fromm, E.: *The Sane Society.* New York, Rinehart, 1955.

*Havelock, R.G.: *The Change Agent's Guide to Innovation in Education.* Englewood Cliffs, NJ, Educational Technology, 1973.

Lewin, K.: *Field Theory in Social Science: Selected Theoretical Papers.* New York, Harper and Row, 1951.

Lippitt, G. L., and Lippitt, R.: *The Consulting Process in Action.* La Jolla, CA, University Associates, 1978.

*Lippitt, G.L.: *Visualizing Change: Model Building and the Change Process.* Fairfax, VA, NTL Learning Resources, 1973.

Lortie, D.C.: Administrator, advocate, or theorist? Alternatives for professionalization in school counseling. In Mosher, R.L., Carle, R.F., and Kehas, C.D. (Eds.): *Guidance, an Examination.* New York, Harcourt, 1965, pp. 127-143.

Paul, M.F.: Power, leadership, and trust: Implications for counselors in terms of organizational change. *Personnel and Guidance Journal, 60*:538-541, 1982.

Schein, E.H.: *Process Consultation: Its Role in Organization Development.* Reading, MA, Addison-Wesley, 1969.

Walz, G.R., and Benjamin, L.: A change agent strategy for counselors functioning as consultants. *Personnel and Guidance Journal, 56*:331-334, 1978.

*Walz, G.R., and Benjamin, L.: *On Becoming a Change Agent.* Ann Arbor, MI, ERIC/CAPS, 1977.

*Wigtil, J.V., and Kelsey, R.C.: Team building as a consulting intervention for influencing learning environments. *Personnel and Guidance Journal, 56*:412-416, 1978.

*Recommended readings

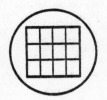

CHAPTER 11

CONSULTING WITH INSTITUTIONS

THIS chapter on institutional consultation is closely linked with the topic of change agentry discussed in Chapter 10. By serving as consultants to institutions, counselors can effect social change, champion human rights, and, at the same time, help institutions improve their organizational structure and productivity. As was mentioned earlier in this volume, there is a high correlation between the welfare of workers and their efficiency in virtually all organizational settings.

Gibbs (1978) makes a parallel point by showing how trust and fear affect organizational environments and the individuals who work there. He proposes the concept of *environmental quality* (EQ), which he classifies on a scale of ten ascending levels: from punitive and autocratic to holistic, transcendent, and cosmic. He argues that any upward movement on the EQ scale benefits both the individuals who work in an organization and the organization itself.

The close correlation of the personal fulfillment of the workers and the organizational development of the institution is the central theme of this chapter. The range of services provided by consultants to institutions is shown in Figure 11-1. On the Three-Dimensional Intervention Model, the services cover the area 3 — A, B, C, D — I, II, III. Although individuals and groups are also addressed in the process of institutional consultation, this occurs only to the extent that they are a part of the organization.

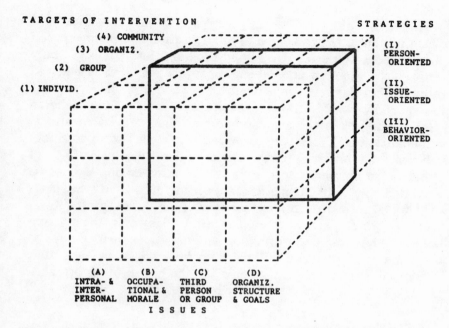

TARGETS OF INTERVENTION

(4) COMMUNITY
(3) ORGANIZ.
(2) GROUP
(1) INDIVID.

STRATEGIES

(I) PERSON-ORIENTED
(II) ISSUE-ORIENTED
(III) BEHAVIOR-ORIENTED

(A) INTRA- & INTER-PERSONAL
(B) OCCUPA-TIONAL & MORALE
(C) THIRD PERSON OR GROUP
(D) ORGANIZ. STRUCTURE & GOALS

ISSUES

Figure 11-1. Consulting with Institutions (Perimeter of Interventions in Solid Lines) within the Three-Dimensional Intervention Model (Dotted Lines).

UNDERSTANDING ORGANIZATIONAL SYSTEMS

To be effective in consulting work with institutions, counselors need to understand the internal structure of organizational systems. In the broadest sense, organizations are associational groups whose members cooperate for the attainment of certain goals and thus have some similarities with socio groups. However, since organizations are usually large and their structure is complex, they do not fully conform to the group definition presented in Chapter 9. Organizations can be defined as dynamic structures, characterized by built-in supervisory mechanisms and by planned cooperation of their members. Members of the organization understand and implement their tasks, which are divided and coordinated for the attainment of envisioned results. The results are then evaluated (Ryan, 1978; Bell and Sirjamaki, 1965).

Lippitt (1969) points to the complexity of most organizations, which results in a high degree of specialization and fragmentation of knowledge and effort. A unified program can be achieved only through coordination and integration processes. This is achieved through the planning, implementing, supervising, and evaluating functions by organizational management. In addition, Halloran (1978) emphasizes the paramount importance of organizational communication. Unless organizational messages are understood, believed, and internalized by the rank and file, little unity of effort or commitment to organizational goals among workers is generated. An enlightened management particularly supports the vertical flow of information between the upper and the lower echelons, which parallels line relationships. However, the horizontal or lateral flow of information among persons and groups at the same level or organizational hierarchy, which parallels staff relationships, is equally important for the health of an organization.

Theory X and Theory Y

McGregor (1960) has developed a well-known theoretical framework for understanding two contrasting approaches to management, known as Theory X and Theory Y. Theory X is based on a negative and pessimistic view of human nature. People are seen as lazy, unambitious, and generally irresponsible by nature. They are not credited with much intelligence or willingness to accept organizational aims as their own. Unable to take initiative and act decisively in goal-oriented patterns, people are perceived as requiring outside direction. On the basis of these premises, managers advocating Theory X promote organizational success by exerting close control over workers. They engage in influencing the behavior of workers by means of persuasion, inducement, rewards, and punishment.

In contrast, Theory Y assumes that it is natural for average people to put effort into projects they understand and are committed to, particularly if they can combine their work with personal satisfaction. Although people have varied degrees of intelligence, they are perceived as capable of doing their jobs and as responsible members of the organization if given the opportunity to express their views and to make recommendations in organizational matters. On the basis of these assumptions, Theory Y managers de-emphasize control mechanisms and rely instead on self-control by workers. They try to provide organizational conditions that will stimulate and release the full potential of workers and promote a conscious and realistic linkage of the workers' personal aims and organizational objectives.

Organizational Health and Illness

Fordyce and Weil (1971) have studied the structure and behavior of organizations in terms of organizational illness and health and have concluded that unhealthy organizations generally "exhibit behavior which would be characterized as immature or pathological in individuals" (p. 8). Their views on the symptomatology of organizational health and illness are contained in twenty-three propositions, which have been summarized around four major themes.

Manager Attitudes

Manager attitudes in unhealthy organizations parallel McGregor's (1960) Theory X, while manager attitudes in healthy organizations generally follow Theory Y. In unhealthy organizations, managers come across as authority figures ("prescribing fathers") who exert control over most decision making, hold little respect for the judgment of people at lower levels, discourage innovation among rank and file, and tend to fall back on organizational traditions.

In contrast, managers of healthy organizations are flexible in their leadership styles; they trust subordinates and promote team work and the sharing of responsibility throughout the organization. They respect the judgment of people lower down and welcome input or innovative initiatives from individuals and groups at any level. They maintain a sense of organizational continuity, but readily question existing methods, which may have outlived their usefulness.

Worker Attitudes

In unhealthy organizations, workers have no personal invest-
ment in the organizational aims. They may not even understand
the aims, and, if they do, they do not identify with them. Workers
see the organization as uninterested in their personal feelings and
needs. They realize that their input is not sought and, when given,
not appreciated. Workers regularly criticize the way things are
done, but feel that they can do nothing to change things for the
better. Under such conditions, people feel bored with their jobs
and trapped in a no-win situation. Edelwich and Brodsky (1980)
consider this frame of mind to be the beginning stage of burnout.

In contrast, workers in a healthy organization understand and
identify with organizational goals. They feel that their personal
needs and values are recognized. They realize that their input, including constructive criticism, is listened to and appreciated. They
have a degree of satisfaction on the job. If things occasionally get
bogged down, they know that mechanisms for changing and
improving the organization are available and do not hesitate to
use them.

Interpersonal Relations

In unhealthy organizations, interpersonal relations lack authenticity. People pretend and play games, particularly in conflict
situations that are covered up and handled through in-house
politics. People tend to feel isolated and vulnerable. They compete
with each other, protect their own turf, and generally look out for
themselves rather than for each other.

In healthy organizations, people feel free to be themselves
and to relate to others (including superiors) without pretense.
When conflicts arise, they are handled in the open. Since frank
discussion is tolerated, people can settle their differences without
holding grudges against each other. Individuals identify with their
group and enjoy team work. They do not feel alone or threatened.
Rather they care for each other and help each other.

Problem Solving and Crisis Management

In unhealthy organizations, problem solving frequently bogs
down because of inflexible attitudes of management that places

priority on procedural matters, such as going through appropriate channels rather than focusing on the essence of the problem. Important aspects of the problem may be avoided for fear that admitting them would offend a supervisor. Workers are anxious not to take unnecessary chances. When a problem develops into an acute crisis, most workers withdraw and refuse to assume ownership of the crisis. They tend to let someone else settle things or to blame each other.

Conversely, in healthy organizations, both management and rank and file focus on the problem rather than on the mechanics for dealing with it. No attempt is made to gloss over unflattering realities, no matter whose sensibilities may be offended. The main emphasis is on finding an equitable solution to the issue. Since workers are involved in team work and cooperate with each other the year around, crisis situations make them band together even more. They usually confront the potential risks inherent in the crisis as a group, but would not hesitate facing such risks individually either.

THE CONSULTATION PROCESS

In every institutional consultation, primary attention should be given to the specific problems (e.g. interdepartmental frictions and absenteeism) that triggered the request for a helping intervention. The solution of such problems is the immediate goal of the consultation project. However, the consultant should view such problems in perspective as indicators of the institution's organizational health or illness. The comprehensive, long-term goal of all institutional consulting work is the improvement of the "macrodesign" of the organization, i.e. its overall structure, coordination, and communication patterns.

At this point, it may be useful to reread the passages explaining the consultation process (Chapter 4) or the change agentry process (Chapter 10). That information will be linked to the organization development approach, which has been used in corporate settings for many years and which is now finding its way into consulting work with educational institutions and mental health agencies.

The Organization Development (OD) Approach

It was stated earlier in this chapter that the behavior of un-healthy organizations closely parallels that of emotionally dis-tubed individuals. By the same token, the behavior of healthy organizations resembles the behavior of well-adjusted people. Fordyce and Weil (1971) further expand on this argument:

> Our approach rests on a fundamental belief that in any organizational setting the individual members must have the opportunity to grow if an ailing organization is to revive or a vital one is to maintain its health. . . . When people work at the tasks involved in a change in such way that their humanness and entirety is engaged along with other known factors, then they themselves recommence to grow. To be treated as an "it," so to treat yourself or others, is to be "busy dying." Besides, it's damned inefficient. On the other hand, to treat respect-fully the person (including oneself) in any problem involving persons is to be "busy being born." Such problem-solving is a remedy for prob-lems and for man (p. 15).*

This forcefully formulated theoretical assumption underlies the entire OD approach. Thus, organization development can be defined as a planned, long-range process for the increase of organizational effectiveness by giving attention to the people who belong to an organization. It is an effort to bring into har-mony the corporate needs of the organization and the personal needs of the workers (French and Bell, 1978; Leonards, 1981). OD has its philosophical roots in social humanism, which in the opinion of Bennis (1969) will eventually lead not only to a more human organizational world, but also to greater productivity.

OD Methodology

Huse (1978) believes that after a period of methodological rigidity, OD has found a balanced approach. The erstwhile over-emphasis in American OD on T-group approaches, whether they were appropriate for the situation or not, has been modified. And the excessive emphasis in European OD on autonomous work teams, which has proven successful in some Scandinavian auto-

---

*From J.K. Fordyce and R. Weil, *Managing with People: A Manager's Handbook of Organization Development Methods*, Reading, MA, Addison-Wesley, 1971. Reprinted by permission of Fordyce and Weil.

mobile plants, has also been corrected. At present, the methodology of OD is manifold and flexible. No single approach or behavioral technology is seen as a prerequisite for successful OD interventions (Goodstein, 1978). For instance, the process and the stages discussed in Chapters 4 and 10 are fully applicable to OD, as long as three basic conditions are met:

1. OD must be a collaborative effort of the consultant, the management, and key personnel in the organization that is to be improved.
2. OD places strong emphasis on the gathering of data. In terms of the three-dimensional intervention model, strategy II (issue-oriented) is to be used as the primary approach.
3. OD is a cyclical process that needs to be carried out long enough to become an ongoing, self-sustained mechanism for organizational renewal within the institution.

Typical Sequence of the OD Process

To provide a better understanding of the OD process, the sequence of seven developmental steps proposed by Huse (1978) is presented here:

1. Identification of the problem by someone in authority within the organization
2. Consultation of organizational representatives with an OD expert
3. Gathering of data and preliminary diagnosis undertaken by the OD consultant through interviews, questionnaires, observation, etc.
4. Feedback by the OD consultant to representatives of the organization and their reaction to the collected data communicating agreement or disagreement
5. Bilateral diagnosis of the problem by OD consultant and organizational representatives, which stimulates commitment by the organization to assume ownership of the problem
6. Joint agreement on an action to be taken and eventual implementation of the action

7. Gathering of data after the action has been taken to assess its impact and outcomes. This leads to a new diagnosis and to an additional action. The cyclical process continues until consultant and representatives of the organization agree that the OD intervention can be terminated.

OD in Perspective

In the course of its almost fifty years of service to corporate clients, the OD movement had a major impact on the organizational climate in many industrial countries of the world. Its accomplishments include the improvement of interpersonal skills, the legitimizing of feelings among people in corporate settings, an increase of intragroup and intergroup understanding, and the strengthening of conflict management processes (Bennis, 1969). OD has also consistently emphasized the principle of team work and the need for involvement of rank and file workers in the affairs of their organizations. Since the early 1960s, OD has become virtually synonymous with organizational change and with change agentry in general.

However, in spite of these accomplishments, humanistic change agents are disturbed by the overly pragmatic attitudes shown by a number of OD adherents. Even OD theorists themselves, such as Burke and Goodstein (1980), admit that some OD interventions merely pave the way for administrators to manipulate change in the direction they have chosen by helping soothe the feelings and erode the resistance of the rank and file: "This boss-directed change may not be bad, of course; but nagging the OD practitioner are several questions: Who is the client? Is my assistance helpful to all involved or just to the boss? Is my job to help the boss or to facilitate system change?" (p. 7).

These concerns, voiced by recognized OD authors, make it clear that the organization development approach is in itself no panacea of social renewal nor a guarantee of protection for human rights. No matter how well suited it is to people-oriented organizational consultation, OD (like any other method or technique) depends for its processes and aims on the values and professional vigilance of the person using it.

PRACTICAL APPLICATIONS

Consulting with Educational Institutions

There are numerous operational manuals and resource books — many of them with strong OD orientation — that offer the institutional consultant a plethora of techniques for individual and group activities, evaluation procedures, samples of questionnaires, etc. (e.g. Fordyce and Weil, 1971; Harvey and Brown, 1976; Woodcock and Francis, 1978). Among the resources for consultation with educational institutions are two books on change agentry by Havelock (1973) and by Walz and Benjamin (1977), quoted in the previous chapter. A major OD-oriented resource is *The Second Handbook of Organization Development in Schools* by Schmuck, Runkel, Arends, and Arends (1977), who call their volume "a guide to change in education written for those who wish to make schools more joyful places for working and learning" (p. xvi).

The few practical suggestions presented here are meant as basic advice for counselors who are entering the field of institutional consultation. In the process of their consulting interventions, novice consultants will benefit by adhering to the following guidelines.

(1) Establish a Broad Base of Operation

Personally meet as many people as possible. Let them talk and listen both for content and feeling in their communication. Do not let management or power groups steer you away from meeting people who may present an unflattering assessment of the organization. When meeting people, be highly person-oriented, using strategy I of the Three-Dimensional Intervention Model. Encourage people to tell you exactly how they feel about the problem under discussion, about their institution in general, and even about their job.

Some people may be tempted to discuss their personal problems; if this happens, remind them tactfully that you will not do individual counseling as part of your consultation, and offer them information on opportunities for personal counseling elsewhere. Assure everyone that confidential information given to you will be fully protected. However, if a person hopes to bring things into the open, he or she must allow you to use information that is relevant to others and to the organization itself. Do not take sides in disputes. If put on the spot, emphasize the need for cooperation: "If we work on this issue together, we are bound to find a solution that will help all of us. None of us should be a loser."

(2) Observe the Flow of Communication

See by what mechanisms or in what manner people and groups communicate within the organization. Is communication generally open and spontaneous or formal and guarded? Do people at meetings typically speak their minds? Are some of them being discouraged from speaking or even cut off? Which forces seem to block communication and which forces seem to stimulate it? Does management relate its messages to the rank and file effectively, and does it seek feedback? What is the quality of intergroup and interpersonal communication at the horizontal level?

(3) Pay Special Attention to Informal Communication and Leadership Systems in the Organization

Communication is a powerful leadership tool within organizational structures. The management establishes and controls a formal communication network that contains a regulated flow of written messages (guidelines, memoranda, questionnaires, etc.), a schedule of regular staff meetings, and provisions for individual conferences of management and staff members.

However, in every organization one can also find an informal communication network that is outside of the administrators' control. People talk with each other while they work and at coffee breaks and they see each other socially after work; during these informal encounters they share their work-related experiences, both pleasant and disappointing, and bits of gossip. Schmuck et al. (1977) have this caution:

> Problems arise when informal communications run counter to formal communications. Most formal communication is followed by interactions in small informal groups that strive to achieve an adequate understanding of the original message. When the original message is distorted by these informal discussions, problems of coordination arise for the organization. When the most influential members of the informal net-

works disagree with the views and decisions of the formal leaders, the messages from the informal leaders often take precedence over the formal communications, a breakdown in authority occurs and norms about decision making become ambiguous, which leads to the development of distrust in a work situation, the more so when differences of opinion and belief are kept private (p. 101).

(4) Examine the Goals of the Organization

In business organizations the goals are clearly related to the profit motive of the operation. However, in educational and human services organizations, the goals are not always clear beyond the general aim of providing *quality education* or *quality service*. Often it is not spelled out what the top priorities and the specific objectives of the organization are (e.g. are they in the area of academic excellence or of psychosocial development?). Also, ambiguity may exist about the most effective means by which objectives of the program or operation will be obtained. Goodstein (1978) points out that poor articulation of institutional goals and methodology may produce unnecessary pressures and anxiety among staff members. In his view, the consultant should elicit perceptions and definitions of institutional goals from various members of the staff and initiate a dialogue on the subject. Even if the goals are clear to members of the organization, they may not be clearly communicated to the public. This, of course, means that the organization is cutting itself off from important sources of support.

(5) Assess the Degree of Job Satisfaction and Staff Morale

Schmuck et al. (1977) summarize the prevalent opinions of people on organizational health and satisfaction of workers as follows:

Most of us believe that a strong, resilient organization that meets internal and external challenges with competence and vigor will be composed of people who come to work in the morning feeling good about their day, and who are in general well satisfied with their lives as part of the organization. Indeed, because work preoccupies so much of our lives, many people believe that being happy on the job is a worthwhile end in itself. For these reasons, many social scientists and industrial psychologists regard the satisfaction of organizational members as a touchstone for organizational health and adaptability. For their part,

OD consultants design interventions for change projects to include activities that bring immediate satisfactions so that participants will be encouraged to continue working toward a more satisfying organization (p. 475).

The suggestion of providing immediate satisfaction for workers — desirable in itself — has to be followed with caution. The consultant has to avoid the trap mentioned earlier in this chapter of artificially soothing the feelings of the workers, thus eroding their resistance to changes premediated or designed by the administration contrary to workers' wishes.

The most satisfying yet genuine results of a consulting intervention, both short- and long-term, are the opening of lines of honest communication between staff members and management and the ensuing feeling among rank and file that they can influence the affairs of the organization. Another highly satisfying result is the knowledge that hard work and competence will be rewarded, particularly if they are combined with a clear mutual understanding between staff members and management as to what is expected from each worker in a given time span.

(6) Assess Problem-Solving and Decision-Making Processes in the Organization

Are problems in the organization solved and decisions made by management, by majority vote, or by a broad consensus of management and staff arrived at after a period of dialogue? Schmuck et al. (1977) define consensus as

a process in which: (1) all members can paraphrase the issue under consideration to show that they understand it, (2) all members have a chance to voice their opinions on the issue, and (3) those who continue to doubt or disagree with the decision are nevertheless willing to give it a try for a prescribed period of time without sabotaging it. Consensus is therefore different from a unanimous vote. It does not mean that everyone agrees or even that the decision represents everyone's first choice; it means that enough people are in favor of it for it to be carried out and that those who remain doubtful nonetheless understand it and will not obstruct its implementation (p. 324).

Since consensus building is perceived by some managers as a threat to their authority, it may become a thorny issue for you as a consultant. You need to help managers experience the added effectiveness of problem solving and the greater commitment to change among the rank and file that result from sharing responsibility for decision making. This is best accomplished if you consistently solicit worker involvement during all phases of the consultation process.

(7) Counselor-Consultant, Be Yourself

While the processes of consultation and counseling are not identical, you, the counselor, will be using the same basic skills in both helping activities. This involves, of course, sensitivity to the demands of each situation and flexibility on your part. However, since the principal instrument in all your helping interventions is your own personality, you owe it to yourself and to your clients to remain true to yourself.

Although you will focus on a broad agenda of the entire organization, you will also deal with individuals and groups using your interpersonal and group leadership skills, as you do in counseling. In the process of consultation you will have to use all three strategies of the three-dimensional intervention model: (a) the person-oriented strategy (I) for helping people deal with their feelings and personal values, (b) the issue-oriented strategy (II) for maintaining objectivity in exploration of existing problems, and (c) the behavior-oriented strategy (III) for social modeling and for reinforcement of behavioral changes.

As a novice consultant, you will be wise to study field techniques and examples of organizational consultation shared by experienced professionals. In addition to the books mentioned earlier in this chapter, literature provides numerous reports on organizational consultation cases (e.g. Dole, Love, and Levine, 1973; Schmuck et al., 1975; Meyers, 1976; Carrington, Cleveland, and Ketterman, 1978; Werner, 1978; Lennox, Flanagan, and Meyers, 1979; Beer, 1980).

Consulting with Industry

While counselors have worked as consultants with schools and school districts for several years, relatively few of them have served as consultants to organizations in the public sector and corporate units in industry. This situation is now gradually changing. Griffith (1980) points out that counselors' services can be valuable to private industry, e.g. for organizing substance abuse rehabilitation programs. Herr and Cramer (1979) suggest consultation opportunities for counselors in the area of career development in the labor force, including occupational reorientation and midcareer changes. These issues, which have increasingly affected industry during the past twenty years, are linked not only to job obsolescence but also to shifts in workers' motivation, values, and personal goals (Clopton, 1973; Entine, 1977). If untreated, career maladjustment leads to lowering of worker morale, interpersonal and intergroup frictions, and eventually to worker burnout (Freudenberger, 1977).

Industrial organizations are also becoming increasingly aware of the needs of older workers who are in the preretirement stage of their careers. Although adjustment to retirement is obviously an individual matter, the transition from job-mandated work to self-selected, postemployment activities can be greatly facilitated by information and support programs provided by the organization. Davidson and Kunze (1965) have documented the existence of such preretirement support programs developed as early as thirty years ago.

Other areas in which counselors can effectively serve industrial units are related to employee problems generated outside of the work environment, such as marriage and family problems, e.g. disabling illness of relatives or bereavement. Although such problems have originated at the worker's home, they have a profound impact on his or her morale and job performance.

SUMMARY

1. To be successful in institutional consultation, counselors have to understand the nature and internal processes of organizational systems.

2. McGregor's (1960) Theory X and Y are helpful aids for understanding basic approaches to management of organizations.

3. Fordyce and Weil (1971) have developed a symptomatology of healthy and unhealthy organizations; the respective organizational processes parallel healthy and pathological behavior of people.

4. Institutional consultation has been interpreted in this chapter primarily in terms of organization development (OD); the theoretical basis, methodology, and relative merits of OD have been explored.

5. To facilitate the entry of counselors into the field of organizational consultation, seven operational guidelines have been proposed for their use.

6. Although counselors serving as organizational consultants frequently limit their work to educational institutions, they possess skills that are equally needed for consultation work in private industry.

REFERENCES

*Beer, M.: *Organization Change and Development: A Systems View.* Santa Monica, CA, Goodyear, 1980.

Bell, E.H., and Sirjamaki, J.: *Social Foundations of Human Behavior,* 2nd ed. New York, Harper and Row, 1965.

Bennis, W.G.: *Organization Development: Its Nature, Origins, and Prospects.* Reading, MA, Addison-Wesley, 1969.

Burke, W.W., and Goodstein, L.D. (Eds.): *Trends and Issues in OD: Current Theory and Practice.* San Diego, CA, University Associates, 1980.

Carrington, D., Cleveland, A., and Ketterman, C.: Collaborative consultation in the secondary schools. *Personnel and Guidance Journal, 56:*355-358, 1978.

Clopton, W.: Personality and career change. *Industrial Gerontology,* (spring): 9-17, 1973.

Davidson, W.R., and Kunze, K.R.: Psychological, social and economic meanings of work in modern society: Their effects on the worker facing retirement. *The Gerontologist, 5:*129-133, 1965.

Dole, R.C., Love, B.J., and Levine, D.V.: Systems renewal in a big-city school district: The lessons of Louisville. *Phi Delta Kappan, 54:*524-534, 1973.

Edelwich, J., and Brodsky, A.: *Burn-out: Stages of Disillusionment in the Helping Professions.* New York, Human Sciences Press, 1980.

Entine, A.: Counseling for mid-life and beyond. *Vocational Guidance Quarterly, 25:*332-336, 1977.

*Fordyce, J.K., and Weil, R.: *Managing with People: A Manager's Handbook of Organization Development Methods.* Reading, MA, Addison-Wesley, 1971.

---

*Recommended readings

French, W.L., and Bell, C.H.: *Organization Development*, 2nd ed. Englewood Cliffs, NJ, Prentice-Hall, 1978.

Freudenberger, H.J.: Burn-out: the organizational menace. *Training and Development Journal, 31(7)*:26-27, 1977.

Gibbs, J.R.: *Trust: A New View of Organizational Development*. Los Angeles, Guild of Tutors Press, 1978.

*Goodstein, L.D.: *Consulting with Human Service Systems*. Reading, MA, Addison-Wesley, 1978.

Griffith, A.R.: A survey of career development in corporations. *The Personnel and Guidance Journal, 58*:537-542, 1980.

*Halloran, J.: *Applied Human Relations: An Organizational Approach*. Englewood Cliffs, NJ, Prentice-Hall, 1978.

Harvey, D.F., and Brown, D.R.: *An Experiential Approach to Organization Development*. Englewood Cliffs, NJ, Prentice-Hall, 1976.

Herr, E.L., and Cramer, S.H.: *Career Guidance through the Life Span*. Boston, Little, Brown, and Co., 1979.

*Huse, E.F.: Organization development. *Personnel and Guidance Journal, 56*:403-406, 1978.

Lennox, N., Flanagan, D., and Meyers, J.: Organizational consultation to facilitate communication within a school staff. *Psychology in Schools, 16*:520-526, 1979.

Leonards, J.T.: Corporate psychology: an answer to occupational mental health. *Personnel and Guidance Journal, 60*:47-51, 1981.

Lippitt, G.L.: *Organizational Renewal: Achieving Viability in a Changing World*. Englewood Cliffs, NJ, Prentice-Hall, 1969.

McGregor, D.: *The Human Side of Enterprise*. New York, McGraw-Hill, 1960.

Meyers, J.: A consultation model to help a school cope with the process of bereavement. *Professional Psychology, 7*:559-564, 1976.

Ryan, T.A.: *Guidance Services: A Systems Approach to Organization and Administration*. Danville, IL, Interstate, 1978.

Schmuck, R.A., Murray, D.G., Smith, M.A., Schwartz, M., and Runkel, M.: *Consultation for Innovative Schools: OD for Multiunit Structures*. Eugene, OR, Center for Educational Policy and Management, 1975.

*Schmuck, R.A., Runkel, P.J., Arends, J.H., and Arends, R.I.: *The Second Handbook of Organization Development in Schools*. Palo Alto, CA, Mayfield, 1977.

Werner, J.L.: Community mental health consultation with agencies. *Personnel and Guidance Journal, 56*:364-368, 1978.

Woodcock, M., and Francis, D.: *Unblocking Your Organization*. LaJolla, CA, University Associates, 1978.

---

*Recommended readings

CHAPTER 12

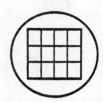

REACHING OUT TO THE COMMUNITY

INSTITUTIONAL consultation and community outreach programs are closely related. It is difficult for change agents to reach the community without using local institutions as stepping stones. For example, counselors involved in community programs need to maintain a positive relationship with agencies under whose jurisdiction the particular areas of the community life fall. Frequently they serve as consultants to agencies and through indirect service help enhance existing programs or formulate new programs for community assistance. At times, this may be burdensome due to bureaucratic restraints, typical of agency functioning. However, in the long run, counselors who are willing to work out their relationship with an agency in a tactful, yet assertive, manner will have achieved a double success. In addition to securing the envisioned community program, they will influence the future policies of the agency and thus act as change agents both for the agency and for the community at large.

Lewis and Lewis (1977) assert the need for direct service to the community, which they call *community counseling*. To make this term better understood, we may want to call it *psychological education for the community*. It is a process of teaching people how to understand themselves and others, how to effectively cope with life's problems, how to grow as persons, and how to succeed in the world of work. However, even this direct community service is best delivered through the consultation approach — by training nonprofessionals to act as helpers — rather than through personal contacts with consumers of the service (Drum and Figler, 1973).

The strategies and steps of consultation and instructional processes and their application to change agentry have been discussed in previous chapters. To avoid belaboring these points, the present chapter does not deal with the process dimension of outreach programs, but explores basic community dynamics and offers practical suggestions for dealing with community issues. A section on evaluating change agentry projects concludes the chapter. In terms of the Three-Dimensional Interventional Model, helping projects for the benefit of the community extend across cells 4 — A, B, C, D — I, II, III, as shown in Figure 12-1.

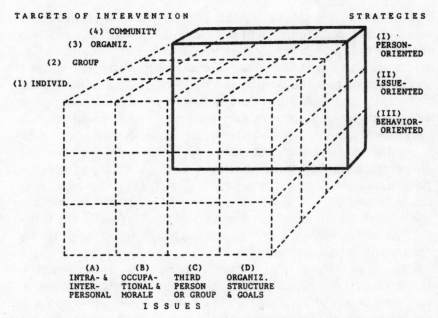

Figure 12-1. Community Outreach Projects (Perimeter of Interventions in Solid Lines) within the Three-Dimensional Intervention Model (Dotted Lines).

THE CONCEPT OF THE COMMUNITY

By definition, the community is a social structure of individuals and primary groups that are located in a determined geographical area. Community members share similar values and goals, are in need of parallel public services, and claim a degree of autonomy and responsibility (Edwards and Jones, 1976). There are many structural similarities between communal and institutional (or industrial) units. However, the formal leadership in the community, at least in American society, exercises a lesser degree of control over the behavior of individuals than does the management of most organizations. There are close parallels between the symptoms of the health (and illness) of a community and that of an organization (*see* Chapter 11).

One of the crucial requirements for healthy community functioning is the unhindered flow of communication between the official leadership (mayor, city council, police department, housing authority, etc.) and the population. Equally important is the flow of communication between various population groups, e.g. the business community and minority groups. A breakdown of vertical or lateral communication produces a feeling of alienation within community groups, stimulates intergroup tensions, and may eventually lead to violence.

Certain authors, e.g. Goode (1957), extend the concept of community to nationwide professional or interest groups, such as the medical profession or the environmentalist lobby. However, in this chapter the focus will be exclusively on the community as a geographical unit.

Interrelation of Institutions and Community

A close interrelation exists between the community and the institutions or organizations that operate there. In the view of Weisbord (1976), the success of any organizational unit largely depends on the support of the social environment in which it exists. No matter how strong the structure of an institution may be, the lack of community support will diminish its effectiveness. The relationship between institutions and community is of major importance for both systems.

The organizational climate of an institution is shaped by the social, ethical, and psychological climate in the community. The prevalent values of the community carry over into the organization through the behavior of local people who work there. Of course, the influence is mutual. For instance, a strong industrial organization has a major impact on the economy and the careers of people in the community. A vigorous human services institution has a similar impact on the life of the community; not only on its economy, but also on the values, the life-styles, and the general behavior of the population, particularly if the community is less than metropolitan in size.

Examples of such behavioral impact can be found in towns where an educational institution, e.g. a state university, is located. Other examples are small cities where a major health institution operates, e.g. Rochester, Minnesota, with its Mayo Clinic, or Topeka, Kansas, the home of the Menninger Foundation. Yet, no matter how large or small a community or an institution may be, the mutual interaction for better or worse is to be recognized as a social reality. By inference, we can assume that the predominant attitudes and values that are found in the community can also be found in local institutions and business organizations.

DEALING WITH COMMUNITY ISSUES

Although the preceding chapters of this volume have provided ample information relevant to counselors' work in a variety of settings, a few specific recommendations are in order for community outreach programs. Counselors should familiarize themselves with three basic processes, which are crucial for the success of such programs:

1. Identifying and using existing community resources
2. Promoting awareness of problem areas where community assistance is needed
3. Making use of the political process for obtaining support for community programs

Identifying Existing Community Resources

Community services programs are needed in many areas of human concerns, ranging from personal growth and life planning to improved housing and economic development of depressed neighborhoods. However, in spite of these multiple needs, it is wise to plan community programs with realistic goals in mind that can be attained by using available resources. Many outstanding community programs originated at the neighborhood level, where they have proven their value. Although small in scope, successful neighborhood programs eventually exert influence on the entire community. On the other hand, overly ambitious projects that are too broad in scope or have unrealistic goals usually fail.

It is always recommended that community workers channel their energy into fields in which they are most proficient. Since by the nature of their professional experiences counselors are well qualified to facilitate human relations and help people develop effective coping behaviors, it is appropriate that they concentrate on these community needs. This does not imply, of course, that they should ignore other needs of the community.

Prior to initiating community work of any kind, the organizers should become familiar with all resources that are available in the community. Fitzsimmons, Sampson, and O'Farrell (n.d.) offer the following classification of agencies and programs that can be tapped as resources in most communities:

1. *Educational Services*

   School districts; schools of all levels and specializations, including vocational and adult education programs, community colleges, and universities; parent-teacher associations; Head Start and Upward Bound programs; etc.

2. *Health Services*

   State, county, and city health departments; public and private clinics; hospitals and community mental health centers; local Red Cross chapters; rehabilitation centers; drug abuse agencies; etc.

3. *Manpower Services*

Public and private employment agencies; unions; skills evaluation centers; neighborhood youth corps; apprenticeship training programs; migrant worker job centers; etc.

4. *Social Services*

Community support agencies such as United Fund, Big Brothers/Big Sisters or YMCA/YWCA; senior citizens centers; halfway houses; churches or church-related social organizations, including Salvation Army and Travelers' Aid; daycare centers; agencies caring for the blind and disabled; social service clubs, such as Parents without Partners; etc.

5. *Economic Development Services*

City urban planning centers; urban renewal programs; state offices of economic development; small business administration units; chambers of commerce; credit unions and financial institutions, etc.

6. *Services Promoting Adequate Housing*

Housing authority offices; urban renewal centers; fair housing committees; Model Cities programs; housing cooperatives, etc.

Using Community Resources

A counselor who wants to engage in community outreach programs cannot operate successfully in isolation. To develop an operational base, he or she should form a team (perhaps seven to ten people) that will serve as an action group for spearheading the community project and for coordinating strategy. As explained earlier (in Chapter 10), the team members should include persons with leadership qualities (although not necessarily formal leaders), members of interest groups, particularly those groups interested in the community needs that are to be addressed, and "gatekeepers," i.e. people who affect the flow of information in the community. Voight, Lawler, and Fulkerson (1980) speak of "networking," as they describe the use of informal channels through which groups in every community exchange ideas and feed information to each other. Obviously, anyone who wishes to influence the community should first seek entry into this network and make use of its communication channels.

Contacts should be maintained with a variety of agencies and groups since their cooperation may be needed — if not immediately, perhaps at a later date. In some communities a directory of available resources and service organizations is regularly published. If no such directory is available, or if the one available contains only certain types of agencies, the counselor should develop and keep current a card file of all relevant community resource groups, including names, addresses, and phone numbers of their leaders.

Promoting Awareness of Community Needs

To pave the way for a community service program, the change agent should prepare the public for it. Such preparation involves the following steps:

1. Promoting awareness of the apparent problem
2. Exploring its wider implications
3. Helping people assume ownership of the problem
4. Stimulating discussion of possible solutions

This is done by working out a master plan within the action group that will assure adequate publicity, such as appearances of group members on local television shows, preparation of releases for newspapers, letter writing to newspaper editors, etc.

Another useful practice is to offer the services of action group members as guest speakers to clubs in the area. Usually it is not wise to make emotional appeals for support and assistance, no matter how worthy the cause and how obvious the need for action may be. It is preferable to use a low-key, factual approach supported by data and to emphasize how the project will benefit the entire community. The ensuing involvement of community members will gradually generate its own momentum, particularly if the project shows promise.

Community Issues Requiring Attention

Community issues that require attention and the respective helping programs vary from one geographical region to another.

The needs should be carefully identified by the use of various diagnostic tools, e.g. direct observation, questionnaires, and interviews with involved persons. What follows is a list (by no means exhaustive) of typical issues and corresponding community programs that have repeatedly emerged in past years throughout the country:

1. *Issues Involving Life-Span Development of the General Population*
   a. Developmental and recreational programs for children and adolescents
   b. Programs for promoting mental health in adult life (marriage and family life, problem solving, dealing with stress, occupational issues, choosing hobbies, etc.)
   c. Informational and support programs for midlife coping (life-style adjustments, career changes, etc.)
   d. Support programs for people facing old age (preretirement planning, developing creative activities in retirement, etc.)

2. *Issues Related to Special Population Groups*
   a. Programs of cultural bridge building between minority groups and the majority population (information, education, support, social activities, etc.)
   b. Programs for the support of homemakers seeking new careers due to divorce, widowhood, or the empty nest syndrome
   c. Programs for the support of physically and emotionally handicapped persons, including programs to foster understanding of the needs of handicapped persons by the community
   d. Programs for promoting community understanding of people of different cultures or unconventional life-styles

3. *Issues Related to Prevention and Remediation*
   a. Programs for substance abuse prevention or treatment
   b. Programs for preventing teenage pregnancy and for dealing with the problems of teenage parenthood

c. Programs for preventing or for dealing with physical and psychological abuse of family members (spouses, children, and aged relatives)

d. Programs for preventing or for dealing with occupational burnout

Making Use of the Political Process

Because of their professional attitudes and priorities, many counselors are not attracted to politics. For most Americans, politicians and politics have acquired a questionable reputation during the 1970s. Since counselor education curricula give little or no attention to political issues, even those that have a direct bearing on the future of guidance programs, it should not be surprising that many counselors are politically uninformed, perhaps even naive. There is, of course, a substantial difference between "playing politics" at one's job and being politically aware or using political action skills for the promotion of socially beneficial programs. No lesser man than Maslow (1977) has called politics "the actualization of the whole of life" (p. 20), and urged all authentic persons to become involved in the political process from the grassroots up.

McDonough (1982) believes that the former political apathy of counselors is diminishing but that much still needs to be done. Active involvement in the political process is not only a civic but also a professional duty for all counselors, especially for those who wish to promote community outreach programs. Herr (1982) points out the fallacy of the view that good programs automatically sell themselves, and he urges counselors to continually document the social benefits of guidance in general and of individual counseling programs in particular. He suggests that this documentation be done in terms of the ethical value, the proven usefulness, and the cost-effectiveness of guidance.

The political process operates at the federal, state, and local level. While all three levels are important for the future of the profession, counseling practitioners involved in community outreach programs need to pay particular attention to state and local political developments. This involves following the major trends emerging in state, county, and city governmental bodies. It also requires a close scrutiny of the stated positions and past performance of various candidates running for office, from the local school board to the county commission, the city council, the mayor's office, and the state legislature. In some communities, concerned citizens have formed forums for nonpartisan evaluation of legislative candidates' personal qualifications and political programs. The League of Women Voters, with its many local chapters, has established an impressive record in this field.

Soliciting Public Support

Counselors who wish to solicit public support for their programs should contact local or state political figures or their aides (some of whom have considerable influence) to explain their cause in person. It is recommended that they bring along a short position paper explaining the nature of the new program, identifying the population group for whose benefit it is intended, stressing its value for the community (e.g. for the prevention of crime and of youth unrest), and stating the program's estimated cost, staffing, and funding needs.

Counselors may also have to testify at a city council meeting or in front of another governmental body, such as the board of county commissioners. Eddy, Richardson, and Erpenbach (1982) offer useful quidelines on how to present such public testimony, some of which are presented here:

1. Witnesses have to be thoroughly knowledgeable about the program that they are supporting by their testimony.
2. Witnesses should also be familiar with the operational procedures of the governmental body that they are addressing.
3. Witnesses should clearly state their professional background and qualifications.
4. Witnesses should project a professional image by their appearance, dress, and general behavior.
5. Witnesses should address their statements to the members of the governmental body, not to the audience, using names and correct titles.

6. Witnesses should make their point with clarity and brevity, concentrating on substantial issues, and be ready to answer questions.

7. Witnesses should avoid antagonistic statements or criticism of persons.

8. Witnesses should summarize their testimony in a brief and compelling statement.

9. Witnesses should have a sufficient number of copies of a written summary statement for distribution to members of the government body, to representatives of the media, and to interested members of the audience.

In conclusion it should be added that political involvement and lobbying activities used by counselors for the promotion of professional programs are in the best tradition of American democracy, which stresses the obligation of citizens to participate in public affairs. Furthermore, through the political process, concerned counseling practitioners promote humanistic goals in public life, thus providing society with the greatly needed service of social renewal, often far beyond the call of duty.

EVALUATING CHANGE AGENTRY PROJECTS

Evaluation of outcomes is an important part of any well-designed program. This is certainly true of consultation projects that are designed to promote changes in the community, in an institution, or in an industrial organization. The program evaluation process is an assessment of the worth, the adequacy, and the effectiveness of a program according to predetermined criteria. Burck (1978) lists four types of program evaluation in terms of (1) content, (2) input, (3) process, and (4) product. This chapter focuses on the fourth type of evaluation, which is related to program outcomes.

Evaluation Strategies

While measuring outcomes of a business venture consists of collecting data on the increase of profit and is a relatively simple operation, evaluating outcomes of change agentry is more complicated. The behavioral changes of personnel in an agency or social innovations in community life have many facets, both overt and covert. Some behavioral domains, such as attitudes and values, which significantly affect long-term outcomes of change agentry, do not lend themselves to the quantification of data.

The classical research design in which behaviors of matched experimental and control groups are compared through pretest and post-test is generally not used in change agentry projects (Goodstein, 1978). An example of a classical research design follows:

$$\text{Experimental Group:} \quad O_1 \ X \ O_2$$
$$\text{Control Group:} \qquad\quad O_3 \quad O_4,$$

In some pilot projects, a simplified experimental design is used in which the pretest and post-test are administered only to the group of consumers of the service to assess their behavioral changes without reference to a control group.

$$\text{For example:} \ O_1 \ X \ O_2$$

However, counselors serving as consultants have other methods available for evaluating the outcomes of change agentry. As has been repeatedly stated in this volume, every well-planned human services program should have a clearly identified goal or a number of interrelated objectives. This may involve the resolution or improvement of an identified problem situation in the community (e.g. high occurence of teenage problem pregnancies in a particular urban subdivision) or the growth of organizational health of an institution attained through better communication and a broader basis for decision making.

In practical terms, evaluation is the process of comparing the observable program outcomes with the program's stated objectives. To what degree have the objectives been attained? What changes or improvements have occurred in the community environment or in the functioning of an organization as a result of the helping intervention?

The Use of Data

The evaluation of outcomes should be based on data obtained through a wide-ranging feedback from individuals and groups affected by the changes. This may include individual interviews, group meetings, or formal questionnaires. Data should also be obtained through direct observation by competent observers who assess the present state of affairs in the client organization or community. In applying these evaluation strategies to educational institutions, Schmuck, Runkel, Arends, and Arends (1977) make some additional points:

> Although conducting interviews and questionnaires at the end of a project will bring interesting information, the most direct route is to observe whether clients are actually doing what you hoped they would be doing: discussing problems in terms of situation, target, and plan; using the systematic problem-solving method in choosing and trying out solutions; probing resources and playfully exercising abilities that are not usually demanded by their jobs; trying out courses of action instead of explaining away problems defensively; regularly assessing the progress of their action plans and testing whether they are going where they wished to go; and periodically reassessing their goals.
>
> In addition to observing whether these things are being done, consultants must judge whether they are being done more often, more judiciously, and more successfully than they were being done before or in greater degree than they are done by those who have not received consultation (p. 483).

OD-oriented authors, e.g. Lippitt (1969), Huse (1978), and Goodstein (1978), identify as one of the main criteria of success in change agentry the likelihood of the renewal process becoming long-range and cyclical in nature and leading to "institutionalization of change." At the completion of the project, this long-term outcome cannot be assessed; it can be merely predicated. For that reason alone, it is important to periodically re-evaluate the outcomes of the renewal project to ascertain its vitality and permanence.

SUMMARY

1. Community outreach programs are usually structured as consultation projects with various institutions, even in cases when

direct service to community members is intended.

2. In order to be successful in community outreach work, counselors need to understand basic community dynamics and the relationship that exists between the community and its institutions.

3. Counselors should also identify and tap community resources. For that purpose a list of community resources available in most locations has been presented.

4. Prior to community outreach programs, counselors should promote public awareness of the need for such programs through personal contacts and through mass media. A list of typical community issues for which outreach programs are needed has been presented.

5. Counselors should be aware of opportunities inherent in the political process for securing support of community programs. Practical suggestions have been offered for personal contacts with political figures and for presenting testimony in front of governmental bodies.

6. Every community outreach program and every organizational renewal project should be evaluated as to its outcomes. Examples of evaluation strategies have been presented, with emphasis on the use of individual and group feedback, surveys by questionnaires, and personal observation.

REFERENCES

*Burck, H.D.: Evaluating programs: Models and strategies. In Goldman, L. (Ed.): *Research Methods for Counselors: Practical Approaches in Field Settings.* New York, Wiley, 1978, pp. 177-201.

*Drum, D.J., and Figler, H.E.: *Outreach in Counseling: Applying the Growth and Prevention Model in Schools and Colleges.* New York, Intext Press, 1973.

*Eddy, J.P., Richardson, B.K., and Erpenbach, W.J.: Strategies for effective legislative testimony in the counseling profession. *Personnel and Gudiance Journal, 60*:608-612, 1982.

Edwards, A.D., and Jones, D.G.: *Community and Community Development.* The Hague, Mouton, 1976.

*Fitzsimmons, J.J., Sampson, B.C., and O'Farrell, M.B.: *Guidance Manual to Providing Neighborhood Services.* Boulder, CO, not dated.

---

*Recommended readings

Goode, W.J.: Community within a community: The professions. *American Sociological Review, 22*:194–200, 1957.

Goodstein, L.D.: *Consulting with Human Service Systems.* Reading, PA, Addison-Wesley, 1978.

Herr, E.L.: Perspectives on the philosophical, empirical, and cost-benefit effects of guidance and counseling: Implications for political action. *Personnel and Guidance Journal, 60*:594-597, 1982.

Huse, E.F.: Organization Development. *Personnel and Guidance Journal, 56*:403-406, 1978.

*Lewis, J.A., and Lewis, M.D.: *Community Counseling: A Human Service Approach.* New York, Wiley, 1977.

Lippitt, G.L.: *Organization Renewal: Achieving Viability in a Changing World.* Englewood Cliffs, NJ, Prentice-Hall, 1969.

Maslow, A.H.: Politics 3. *Journal of Humanistic Psychology, 17*:5-20, 1977.

McDonough, P.J.: Introduction: Political awareness in the counseling profession. *Personnel and Guidance Journal, 60*:593, 1982.

Schmuck, R.A., Runkel, P.J., Arends, J.H., and Arends, R.I.: *The Second Handbook of Organization Development in Schools.* Palo Alto, CA, Wayfield, 1977.

Voight, N.L., Lawler, A., and Fulkerson, K.F.: Community-based guidance: A "Tupperware party" approach to midlife decision making. *Personnel and Guidance Journal, 59*:106-107, 1980.

Weisbord, M.: Organizational diagnosis: Six places to look for trouble with or without a theory. *Group and Organization Studies 1,* pp. 430-447, 1976.

---

*Recommended reading

AUTHOR INDEX

203

SUBJECT INDEX